I0824055

In My Mindful Era

90 Days to Focus Your Mind, Practice Presence, and Embrace Every Moment

In My Mindful Era

Published by Harper Celebrate, an imprint of HarperCollins Focus LLC.

Cover design and art direction by Tiffany Forrester
Interior design by Kristen Sasamoto
Photography by photosky99/Adobe Stock (vi)

ISBN 978-1-4002-5240-4 (HC)
ISBN 978-1-4002-5249-7 (ePub)

Printed in Malaysia

26 27 28 29 30 PJM 5 4 3 2 1

Contents

Introduction

If you're reading this book, chances are you're a busy person. Your mind is, quite literally, full—crammed with social obligations, work deadlines, TikTok dances, and the lyrics to whatever movie soundtrack your toddler currently has on repeat. There's a lot going on up there. And lately, you can't seem to find a moment to pause and enjoy what's going on around you.

Whether you're leading a huge client meeting, defending your thesis, or planning a showstopping first birthday party, you've been encouraged to have, do, and be it all. To everyone. At all times.

Really, what you have is a racing mind, elevated heart rate, and an inbox with a number of unread emails so far from zero that you're thinking about just deleting the whole thing and starting over.

Your mind may be full, but you're the opposite of mindful. Instead, you push yourself to get things done, missing out on the moment at hand as you count down the minutes to the next mindless social media scroll, mindless snack session, or mindless binge-watch. Seeing a pattern here?

There's no sugarcoating it: Breaking this cycle takes intention. That means *choosing* mindfulness. The word *mindfulness* may sound like your mind is going to get even *more* full, but the exact opposite is true. Practicing mindfulness means taking a pause (even when it feels like there is no time for one) and bringing yourself back to the present moment so that you can truly experience the world around you.

If you're ready to hit "pause" on your to-do list and take time for yourself to find a new era of mindfulness: Welcome. For ninety days, devote time to becoming a more present, mindful version of yourself.

IN THIS BOOK YOU'LL:

- **Learn the power of taking a pause.** It's not your fault that your mind is on approximately one million things—that's what our culture encourages! Endless scrolling through social media, overflowing inboxes, overcommitted calendars, and overall busyness and burnout make it hard to tap into what you're truly feeling, let alone take time to be mindful. You'll practice taking a pause so you can lead a more mindful existence.
- **Practice, practice, practice.** They say it makes perfect . . . and they're not wrong! Over the next ninety days, you'll practice mindfulness by completing activities that encourage you to slow down and take the time to come back to the present moment, so you can refocus your thoughts on what really matters to you.
- **Get vulnerable.** This book works as hard as you do, which means it's up to you to get real with yourself about how you feel, what you're prioritizing, and how to overcome what's keeping you stuck in a cycle of burnout and fatigue.
- **Become more present.** By setting aside a few minutes per day to practice mindfulness and engage with the moment you're in *right now* (don't worry, we'll tell you how to do this), you'll lay the foundation for less scattered and more intentional days ahead.
- **Gain confidence.** We believe in you (you did pick up this book, after all!), and soon you'll believe in yourself. As you go through each day's prompts and activities, you'll get better and better at coming back to the present moment, grounding yourself, and slowing down.

Enter your mindful era. Complete this sentence: *A more mindful me is:* ______________________________.
No matter how you choose to define it, you can achieve a more relaxed, caring, considerate, and present version of yourself by committing to it every day.

THIS BOOK PAIRS WELL WITH:

A journal and something to write with. Whether you use a pen or pencil, a leatherbound notebook, or the hodgepodge time capsule that is your Notes app, you should create a space to record your journey. Writing down what you're thinking and feeling is a great way to track your progress (because there will be progress). In addition, there will be occasional writing prompts to guide your thoughts or a specific activity for you to complete. And trust us: You'll want to keep track of it all.

An open mind. This book *is* about mindfulness, after all. Many of the activities in here encourage you to open your mind to the sights, sounds, feelings, and even smells around you. Keep your mind and heart open to the possibilities. When you come to each day's activity, try your best (no matter how silly the activity may seem), and remember to be kind to yourself.

That's all you need. Well, that and a few minutes a day to focus on becoming a more mindful version of yourself.

LET'S GET STARTED, FRIEND!

Your Mind, Your Business

Mind your business? No, bestie. Your mind *is* your business. And we're so proud of you for taking care of business like the absolute boss you are. The first step: starting your mindfulness journey. Look at you go!

Mindfulness is all about coming back to the present so that you can live in the moment and enjoy the world around you. The next ninety days will be about stepping into that truth: When you make your mind your business, you can transform the way you walk through the world. You'll find peace in the present, joy in the small moments, and contentment in your day-to-day life. All it takes is reminding yourself that you're the boss.

While this may not seem true sometimes, you are in control. You have the power to pause. No matter how quickly your thoughts are racing, or the world is moving around you, you are the boss. You can decide, at any point, that you prefer to slow down, take in what's happening around you, and be present with the people you care about in the places you love.

THE BOSS TAKES INVENTORY

Open your notebook, grab something to write with, and take an inventory of what typically distracts you or pulls you out of the moment. Some common distracters might be social media (and the need to constantly scroll), anxiety about something going on in your life, a long list of goals and tasks you need to accomplish, or even people around you who are all too capable of providing a distraction. Committing these things to paper helps you see them more clearly as you move through this mindfulness journey.

My mind is mine; I am in control.

Eyes on the Prize

At the end of every race is a finish line, and at the start of every race is the reason for running it. Let's say you're training for your first-ever 5K. You've got the gear, you've downloaded an app to help you train, you've plotted your route. But what gets you out the door?

No matter all the material prep you do, your motivation will always come from within. A pair of expensive sneakers won't force you to get up and run when it's raining outside. Instead, you need to look inward to figure out why you're running in the first place.

This is true with any journey. You may have picked up this book, bought a new set of pens, and cracked open a new journal. But getting clear on *why* you're opening this book every day will help you, well, open this book every day.

When you find your "why," you'll discover that there is more motivating you than you ever thought possible. So push past the surface-level stuff. Dig deeper to find out if there's a hidden motivation that'll teach you something new about yourself.

DEFINE YOUR "WHY"

You picked up (or were gifted) this book for a reason: You want to cut through the noise of your day-to-day life, stop feeling so overwhelmed and dysregulated, and become more present. Now, the question to ask yourself is: Why? *In your notebook, write down* why *you've decided to practice mindfulness. Try to keep your words positive, and don't be hard on yourself. Then, as you sift through all of the reasons you picked up this book, you'll find your "why," and you can focus on it to center yourself.*

I can form a positive mind-set around my goals.

Be Your Body's Bestie

Think about your best friend or someone you consider very close to you. Picture them standing in front of you. We bet you can conjure up an image of them in your mind: their posture, the clothes they're wearing, their hairstyle, the smell of their favorite perfume or cologne. You know them so well and care about them so much. In the same way, it's important to know and understand your own body.

When you take the time to consider your body—how it moves, what it looks like in the mirror, how it aches after activity—you can immediately tell when something isn't quite right with it. If someone put a wig on your best friend, you'd quickly notice the difference. That's how familiar we'd like your body to become to you.

When you're feeling overwhelmed or anxious, try to check in with your body. Explore where you're holding tension and where you're relaxed. Take your time, and focus entirely on physical sensation. Don't be afraid to investigate how you feel. You'll learn something about yourself in the process.

I can investigate how I feel, little by little.

SCAN YOUR BODY

Find a place to lie down or sit comfortably. Rest your hands in your lap or on your belly and close your eyes. Starting with your toes, take the time to observe any sensations you're feeling. Maybe you feel things like the fabric of your clothing, an itch, or muscle tightness. Gradually, move your attention up your body to the top of your head. Where are you holding tension? Notice sensations without judgment as you scan. You can repeat this exercise when you're feeling overwhelmed or out of control.

Close the Tabs

Some days, you're an internet browser with too many tabs open. You start off, for example, searching for something work-related, but then that search has you opening a new tab to look up something different. And before you know it, *that* tab reminds you to open another tab to check your email and . . . you see where we're going. Before you know it, you're off task, trying to get back to where you started, and *everything* takes a little longer to load as a result.

Closing the tabs and starting over can feel difficult, but this can also feel incredibly freeing. And closing the tabs doesn't have to be an all-or-nothing exercise. You can save the ones that are important to you and choose to close out of everything else. If you've found something once, you'll find it again. You have the agency to press pause.

What would happen if you closed your metaphorical tabs and focused on one thing at a time, without allowing yourself to get distracted by what is new or next? We bet you'd feel more connected to now, and a whole lot less anxious in the meantime.

MASTER SINGLE-TASKING

While you're going about your day, choose to focus on one task at a time. You don't need to clean the entire house in the next five minutes. You don't need to take a meeting while you send an email. Close all of your extra tabs (figuratively and literally) and choose to devote your attention to the task at hand. This may feel difficult at first, but don't give up!

I can focus on one thing at a time.

Breathe It In

Breathing is an action we often do mind*less*ly, but what if we told you that breathing is one of the keys to unlocking a more mindful life?

Your breath is your constant companion and an incredible resource on this journey that you can always return to, no matter where you are or what's going on. You breathe in and out all day and night. That means breathing is a great place to start when you feel the need to center yourself—you're already a pro at it, after all! When you feel out of control, you can return to your breath, devoting attention to the rise and fall of your chest, feeling the sensation of air flowing into your lungs then out of your nose or mouth.

Paying attention to your breath gives you a natural rhythm to focus on. As you do, you may find yourself feeling more relaxed, and your heart rate might lower. Focused breathing also connects you back to your physical body, giving you space to explore the sensations you are feeling before moving along to the next project or task.

INHALE THE MOMENT

Focus on how breathing really *feels. Take a deep inhale, feeling the air flow through your nostrils and into your lungs. (You can even place a hand on your chest or belly—or both!—to help you focus on the feeling.) Pause a moment. Then breathe out slowly, feeling your lungs deflate, your chest fall, and the air come out of your nose or mouth. Simply observe, and allow the rhythm to relax you. Repeat as necessary.*

I can count on my breath to ground me.

See It All

I spy with my little eye, someone who is . . . kicking butt and creating a more mindful life for themself. Surprise! It's you.

The sense of sight is powerful. It helps us understand the world around us. When you are practicing mindfulness, it's important to take in the things around you *without* judgment—and *with* a healthy dose of curiosity. Try to view things not just on the surface level. Get closer, go deeper, and explore more thoroughly.

The more specific you get about your observations, the easier it is to keep your mind from wandering. If you see a tree and notice simply, *That's a tree*, there's nothing to stop your next thought from sliding into, *I'm nervous about my son starting kindergarten*. However, if you see a tree and stop to wonder at the roughness of the bark, the light filtering through the leaves, and what critters might call it home, then you stay mindfully in the present. And that's a win!

Getting curious about what you see can ground you in the present and give you permission to linger in the moment as you observe the world around you.

I can focus on the wonder of my surroundings.

I (WELL, YOU) SPY

You don't need a partner to play this classic children's game. Pause for a few moments to take in your surroundings. Play a game of "I Spy" with yourself. Get really specific. For example, don't just say you see a bird; notice the bird's colors and feathers. Think about where the bird might be going and why. This is a great way to encourage yourself to notice the small things around you that bring wonder and joy.

Feel It All

With a long to-do list and a ton on your plate, you might be tempted to block your feelings from your brain. After all, if you don't have any feelings, you don't have to deal with them, right? How clever.

Uh, wrong!

When you block yourself from feeling the full breadth of your emotions, you don't just stop yourself from fully feeling the messy ones, like grief, anger, sadness, or rejection. You also stop yourself from fully feeling the positive ones, like joy, gratitude, calm, and acceptance. Whoops.

Truly *feeling* your emotions can be intimidating or scary. But life is all about experiencing them! When you allow yourself to connect to what's coming up for you in the moment, rather than trying to race ahead or ignore those things, you give yourself permission to feel them—to feel everything.

When you find yourself shutting down in the name of saving time or being more productive, remember to take a moment to pause and ask yourself: *What am I really feeling? How could acknowledging this emotion help me move through it?*

NAME AND CLAIM

Find a place to sit comfortably in (relative) silence and close your eyes. After taking a few deep breaths, take some time to get specific about what you are feeling—or how you've been feeling lately. Is contentment settling into your bones? Are you stressed about something you're not *doing while completing this exercise? Something else? Identify your emotions without any judgment. Allow yourself to acknowledge them and accept them. Emotions are meant to be felt, not feared.*

I do not fear my emotions. I embrace them.

Listen Closely

Hearing is not the same as listening. Hearing is something you do without thinking; sounds simply enter your ears, and your brain registers them. But listening is an active task. To listen, you must pay attention to absorb the words or sounds happening around you. When you actively listen, you give yourself the opportunity to learn something new. It just takes a little effort.

When thoughts are whirling around inside your head, choosing to listen to what's going on *outside* of it can feel more like a chore than an opportunity. "Huh?" and "Can you repeat that?" are common refrains from someone with too much on their mind. Here's a pro tip: If you find yourself asking your bestie a question only to realize you forgot to listen to their answer, it may be time for a reset.

Choosing to listen closely to the world around you gives you the chance to connect more deeply with the people, places, and things in it. There is so much to learn about yourself, your relationships, and the unknown. What can you hear when you truly listen?

THE HEAR AND NOW

Go for a walk outside with the intent of truly listening to your surroundings. Take in the sounds of the leaves rustling, a car driving by, or a dog barking. If you can't make it outside today, then take a moment to sit in the quiet of your home or office and try to hear even the softest of sounds. Notice the things you hear when you're truly paying attention, grounding yourself in the present.

When I stop and listen, I hear so much more.

Cheer Yourself On

Stress, overwhelm, and burnout do two things really well: They steal you from your joy, and they diminish your accomplishments. That's because they keep you looking ahead to an unknowable future (or worse, at *other* people's journeys). You become focused on what *could* happen or what you *should* do. And you know what? All that worrying makes any finish line you cross feel insignificant. You're looking too far ahead to notice what you've accomplished.

When this happens, it's easy to start speaking negatively to yourself, rather than celebrating who you are right now. But instead of being your own worst critic, what if you become your own best cheerleader? We're talking stereotypical, high school rom-com–level—comically loud and unapologetically excited about brilliant, wonderful *you*.

Here's where to start: Just be present. If you're too focused on someone else's path, you'll wander away from where *you* need to go. So be your best supporter and take a mindful pause, consider the path ahead, and set markers for where you'll celebrate. Then cheer yourself on one step at a time. We'll be doing the same!

I can encourage myself through every stage.

MIND YOUR MARKERS

What's something you're working on right now that's stressing you out? It can be something as tangible as a work project (something with lots of parameters already set), or something more abstract like becoming a better friend or partner (which looks different for everyone). Now create your markers for success. Write a timeline and set some goals. Make the timeline as detailed as possible. Set dates in the calendar. Find the moments worth pausing to celebrate, and cheer yourself on.

A Clean Space

You've probably heard about the correlation between a clean space and a clear mind. Well, it's true! Even if we'd prefer that messiness didn't affect us so that we could do whatever feels more pressing instead of cleaning (whether hitting a work deadline, scheduling a doctor's appointment . . . or binge-watching the latest season of *Love Is Blind*).

If you're surrounded by clutter, you may find it difficult to focus on anything else. Trying to prepare a presentation when tumbleweeds of cat hair are rolling across your floor and your brain is screaming, *Laundry! Laundry!* is not only almost impossible, but attempting to ignore your nagging brain adds to your stress.

Meanwhile, a clean and tidy space is a much more peaceful place to exist. A brain that's not stimulated by a chaotic space allows you to focus more easily. Not to mention, have you ever finished cleaning a room and lit an "I cleaned!" candle after? The sense of accomplishment is unmatched.

Do yourself a favor: Tidy up your space so that you can tidy up what's going on in your mind. We promise it's worth it.

TIMER TO TIDINESS

Set aside fifteen minutes today to clean one space in your house. Set a timer and have at it! Try to tackle areas where you work or hang out often, but know that the world—or your home, actually—is your oyster. For extra motivation, play some music or your favorite podcast while you clean, or take before-and-after photos to see how well you did. You can do this a few times per week, once a day, multiple times per day—anytime it suits you!

A clean space helps me to think more clearly.

It's All Strange

Have you ever thought about what it would be like to explain your job to an alien who just landed on Earth? You'd probably say something like: "Well, I take a giant metal tin on wheels to a large building where I sit on a chair (also with wheels) and talk to my co-workers using mail that travels through time and space . . ." You get the gist.

So often, we allow our fears, anxiety, worries, and busyness to get in the way of seeing just how special our lives are. When we've been in the same routine for some time—and especially when we're stressed or dealing with burnout—we can sort of lose our luster. The things that once made our day-to-day feel shiny and new are suddenly nothing to write home about.

But what if we looked at every seemingly "normal" experience in our lives from a different angle?

When you take in the present moment and imagine explaining the situation to someone who has never experienced it before, your perspective shifts. And suddenly, you may find you're able to feel gratitude for your everyday experiences.

ACT LIKE AN ALIEN

The next time your stress is stopping you from being present, or your day-to-day life feels like a burden, try describing it to an alien. You can do this by talking out loud (we're not responsible for the strange looks you'll get if you do this in public!) or by writing it down. Describing your experience to a total outsider gives you the opportunity to discover something new about your circumstance. Suddenly, what you were taking for granted may seem interesting, new, and even a little silly—which might inject some joy and gratitude into your day.

There is always something new to experience.

What's Your Body Saying?

Have you ever noticed that, when you're feeling stressed or anxious, your mind has *no* problem telling your body how to feel? It makes your heart race, your palms sweat, your stomach churn. Here's something to remember: Your body is perfectly capable of telling its own story. Your job is to listen to it early and often.

The soreness between your shoulder blades, the pain in your jaw, the exhaustion at the end of the day: These physical feelings are trying to tell you something. When you clear your mind and focus on how you feel physically, you can better understand your needs. The tension in your neck might be telling you, "Hey, you've been sitting at your computer for too long. Time to take a break." The pain in your jaw could be saying, "Hmm, you seem stressed. How can we remedy that?" When you're overwhelmed, your body responds accordingly. Can you take a pause and allow yourself to feel what your body's telling you?

The better acquainted you are with your body, the easier it is to take physical cues and turn them into mindful moments.

My body tells the story of my circumstances.

LISTEN AND LEARN

Sit down in a comfortable spot. Starting at your head and neck, begin to pay attention to your body. As you explore, notice any tension you are feeling. Common spots are your jaw, neck, and shoulders. Each time you find a tension point, actively try to release it. You can do this by flexing and unflexing the muscles or by shaking your body out. Move your attention through the rest of your body, and release any tension you're holding. Don't judge yourself for being tense—just do your best to resolve it!

Be Nosey

When you're trying to reconnect with your environment and stop an anxiety spiral, your five senses are your greatest assets. They allow you to experience the world through what you see, hear, touch, taste, and smell—and this can help ground you in the *now*.

When it comes to reconnecting with the present, being nosey is a powerful tool. No, we don't mean eavesdropping on someone else's conversation. Although now that we've mentioned it . . . that could be something to try too. Just kidding! We're talking about using your actual nose.

Your nose is constantly informing you of the world around you. It has the ability to surprise, delight, and disgust. Smells are even known to evoke certain memories and emotions. When you can't smell, it impacts your taste, making foods taste bland or just plain wrong. Your nose is an incredible investigator.

When you're feeling overwhelmed or stressed and want to find something to focus on, take a big sniff. Allow the smells around you (hopefully they're pleasant ones) to place you back into your surroundings. After all, your nose always knows.

AROMA THERAPY

Ground yourself in what you can smell. Take a deep breath, wherever you are, and get specific about what you are smelling. Are you picking up the scent of fresh rain? Someone heating up their lunch in the office? A new perfume you love? Use your ability to smell to ground yourself in the world around you, as you investigate what is happening in your space. Name these smells (either in your mind or on a sheet of paper) and explore the ways they surprise and delight you.

My senses anchor me to the world around me.

In Full Bloom

When you've planted something beautiful in your garden, there's a big chance you'll need to do some pruning pretty soon. Pruning involves cutting pieces of a plant away, whether to get rid of dead or dying parts, to train the plant to create a certain shape, or to improve the number of blooms.

Snipping blooms and branches from living plants can feel unfair or even counterintuitive. After all, the reason you plant something is to watch it grow, not to cut it down. Sometimes, though, a good trim is exactly what something needs to flourish. Rosebushes, for example, are often pruned, and the very act of cutting away allows the plant to bloom even more.

Do you see where we're going with this? Friend, your mind is a lush garden, full of thoughts and beliefs (and sure, random song lyrics from 2012). What do you need to prune today? What thoughts are taking you out of the moment and keeping you from the present? Grab the gardening shears because it's time to snip away the thoughts that aren't helping you thrive, so you can experience life in full bloom.

PRUNE THE GARDEN

You'll need paper, scissors, and something to draw with. On a piece of paper, use your drawing tools to make a garden of flowers out of the thoughts running through your head. Each flower represents a thought. When you're finished, look at the paper again and identify the thoughts that are not serving you (or worse, are keeping you from being mindful). Snip off what doesn't serve you so that you can let other thoughts that are more positive grow in their place.

I will make space for good things to flourish.

Make a Conscious Choice

Nobody tells you that being an adult is essentially making decision after decision, big and small. Every. Single. Day. There's no one telling you what to do—you're the boss, and you're understaffed.

On any given morning, you have seemingly endless choices to make. Do you go to the gym or get more beauty rest? Drink coffee at home or buy an eight-dollar latte? Listen to an audiobook or the morning news? Wave to your neighbor or ignore them?

With so many decisions to make, it can be easy to fall into a pattern of making the same choice, day after day, to spare yourself from thinking. However, the best choices are the ones you make thoughtfully. This doesn't mean that each thoughtful choice is always the most "responsible" one; you can *choose* to nap, and we'll cheer you on! But it's good to check in and make sure that *is* the choice you want to make.

By taking a conscious, mindful pause before each decision, you give yourself time to see your options more clearly and to choose the path that sets you up for success, whatever that looks like today.

DON'T PUT IT DOWN; PUT IT AWAY

We're not trying to sound like your parents, bestie, but here's your job for this week: Don't put something down that you can simply put away instead. It sounds simple enough, but if you pay attention to your choices, you'll see how often you choose the convenience of putting something down instead of putting it where it belongs. When you choose to put the object in its rightful place, you are staying present and *making a choice you'll thank yourself for later: a win-win!*

I can always make a thoughtful choice.

Set It in Slo-Mo

Have you ever seen a too-good-to-be-true, out-of-this-world sports play? (Don't worry, this is probably the first and last time we'll bring up sports.) We're talking about the kind of play where one minute, you're taking a bite of your hotdog and the next, everyone around you is on their feet cheering. You try to catch up and see what happened, but everything on the field is moving too fast for you to see clearly. It isn't until the moment is replayed in slow motion that you can see, second by second, how extraordinary the play was.

Your anxious mind has a lot going on. No wonder it feels like you're totally fine one second and completely stressed out the next. You can't follow the ball (it's okay, you tried!), and you feel completely lost.

Lucky for you, you're not a professional athlete. You can hit "pause" at any time. You can ask for a replay. You can move through your task with deliberate slowness in order to connect with the moment you're in. Go on, set *now* in slow motion. See how it changes your perception.

When I slow down the moment, I appreciate it more.

INSTANT REPLAY

After a positive moment in your day, take time to do a quick, sports-style instant replay for yourself. If you're able to do this soon after the positive moment, that's great! You can also do this in the evening, going over your day before bed. Sit in the positive moment for just a bit longer, slowing down the parts that made you feel extra good and replaying them in your mind.

Get Grounded

Getting bogged down with anxiety and overwhelm can make you feel like you're standing on top of a large sand dune. Every move you make, no matter how big or small, causes the ground to shift. Suddenly, you're not only worried about the things around you or the problems you're having; you're also thinking about whether you can rely on the ground to stay firmly beneath your feet! Something that should be a given becomes unstable and uncertain, and this lack of stability can make you even more anxious.

Practicing mindfulness feels a lot like making the decision to step off the dune in favor of solid ground. Doing this doesn't guarantee you'll never experience uncertainty or stress again. But it *does* mean you can always rely on the steadiness a firm foundation provides.

In life you'll tread many types of ground. But there's one tool you have to ground yourself with that allows you to create your own foundation: your feet. They walk you (literally) through the world, and they're a powerful tool for your mind to focus on when you're feeling stressed or anxious.

STAND UP FOR YOURSELF

Stand or sit with your feet (preferably barefoot, but shoes are fine) hip-width apart. Close your eyes and feel your feet on the ground. Wiggle your toes. Rock forward and then backward onto your heels. Lean to the left and then to the right. Take a few deep breaths. With every exhale, imagine you're sending energy to your feet. Feel them firmly anchored to the ground. Remind yourself that you always have the option to ground yourself.

When my mind is wandering, I can stand firm.

DAY 18

Help Yourself to Some Habits

Life is made up of little habits. You may be thinking, *Not mine! I'm terrible at creating habits.* First of all, it's day eighteen of this book, and you're still here, crushing it. Second (and we hate to break this to you), but even your less desirable habits are still habits.

Your day-to-day is proof that you *can* make and keep habits. Think of all of the things you do in the morning. You shower, brush your teeth, make coffee, grab your keys off the hook where you placed them the night before (or spend a few minutes each morning looking for your keys because you have a *habit* of setting them down in random places).

Mindfulness is a habit just like any other. It's a choice to slow down when life begins to feel stressful. It's a choice to take a few deep breaths when you feel yourself becoming anxious. It's a choice to return to the present moment. As you make these choices repeatedly—just like putting your keys on a hook by the door—eventually the habit sticks.

STACK 'EM AND STICK 'EM

A great way to make and keep habits is by stacking them onto already established habits. For example, you might clear the dishwasher while your coffee brews, or you might work out while your laundry is running. How can you stack mindfulness into your day? Are there moments when you can try to take a deliberate pause to breathe or complete another exercise you've learned? Remember, it takes about thirty days or so to form a habit, so practice is the name of the game!

The work will get easier as I form habits.

DAY 19

Look Up

When you're a child, you spend a whole lot of time looking up. Do you remember cloud gazing? As clouds drifted by, you watched them take shape before your very eyes and pointed them out to your friends to see if they were able to see what you saw. A bunny here, an airplane there, a dog, a cat, a boat—you let them float past you, not judging yourself for the shapes you saw, but instead boldly proclaiming what you witnessed. You may have even taken the time to explain to your friends, "See? There are the ears, and there's the tail." You'd point confidently, urging others to see what you did.

Your thoughts and feelings are a lot like those clouds. They roll on through, and sometimes you're able to understand them easily and immediately. Other times, you need to pause and turn your head this way and that to know what you're looking at.

You can always sit up and acknowledge your thoughts, but you can also choose to let them roll on by. There will always be more to look at and experience.

HEAD IN THE CLOUDS

It's time to pause and let the world fill you with wonder, to flex your imagination muscles that perhaps you haven't used in a while. Step outside and look up at the clouds (or rain puddles or shadows, if you don't have a good day for cloud gazing). Dare yourself to cloud gaze, taking time to find shapes in the seemingly shapeless. You can even snap a photo of your favorites to look at later and remind yourself you have a child-like imagination and can take your time.

I can find whimsy in unexpected places.

Embrace the Quiet

Have you ever been driving and turned down the car stereo because you wanted to see better? It seems silly. (Why would audio input affect your eyesight? Music has certainly never dulled our tastebuds!) But it points to a very real truth: The noise around us creates endless distraction, and if we're not careful, that distraction can start to affect the way we see things.

With all kinds of media at your fingertips, you never have to experience silence if you don't want to. You can slip on your headphones and listen to everything but your own thoughts. You can pay attention to anything other than what's right in front of you.

But silence is powerful. In many cases, it communicates just as much as a conversation. When you allow yourself to experience a quiet moment, you can hear yourself and others so much better and become more mindful in the process. Silence gives you space to concentrate on the task or conversation at hand so that you can truly hear and understand what's going on around you. What would happen if you trained yourself to embrace the quiet?

In silence, I can hear myself.

SIT IN SILENCE

Maybe your schedule makes finding a moment alone difficult, but you truly need only seconds to ground yourself. Start small (with the intention of building your way up) by devoting fifteen seconds of your busy day to sitting in silence. This means no music, TV, or phone. Sit in that silence, focusing on your breathing. As you breathe in and out, thoughts may pop up. Silence those stray thoughts by acknowledging them and letting them go.

Let's Table That

Food is one of life's greatest pleasures, but when was the last time you sat down and truly enjoyed a meal? Can you remember when you last took an extra moment to taste and savor the food you were eating? Stress and overwhelm have a way of creeping into even the most unexpected areas of your life. That's because when you're rushing through life, *everything* becomes rushed.

We've all been there: stressed, cranky, and looking for something to eat. Maybe you were even so busy, you skipped a meal. Cue the ravenous hunger! Suddenly, you're standing at the kitchen counter, eating a "girl dinner" that includes a bunch of random ingredients, very little thought, and probably not enough chewing (hello, heartburn!). And hey, girl dinner has its time and place, but this book is all about making you *more* mindful. So let's strive to put a little bit more thought into it!

A simple way to incorporate mindfulness into your day is during meals. Make each meal an experience to savor. Choose your favorite foods and eliminate distraction (no mealtime scroll sessions allowed—sorry!), so you can truly enjoy the experience.

INVESTIGATE YOUR FOOD

The next time you sit down for a meal, choose whatever food you'd like to savor and take time to focus completely on it. But here's the kicker: The more everyday or "boring" food you choose, the more fun and eye-opening this challenge will be! Look at the food's size, color, and smell. Touch it to see what it feels like. Then take a bite. Is it crunchy? Soft? Tart? Sweet? As you slowly chew, think about the food you're eating. Spend time truly enjoying it without rushing. Who knew an apple could be so interesting?

I can eat mindfully and savor the sensation.

Get To, Not *Have* To

Have you ever caught yourself feeling obligated to do something you used to enjoy doing? When you're burned-out and exhausted, it's easy to become resentful. Activities you once did with excitement become just another thing you *have* to do. People you loved to hang out with become people you *must* hang out with.

When you feel resentment bubbling up, that's your reminder to take a break. Hit "pause" and center yourself on this truth: You don't *have* to do this—you *get* to do this. You could have declined the invitation, you could have skipped the event, but here you are. How lucky are you?

In these moments, return to gratitude. Expressing thankfulness for a busy schedule may not feel intuitive, but it'll get easier with practice. Taking a moment to be thankful for the people you love, the setting you're in, the music that's playing, the laughter you're sharing is like a balm for the overwhelmed mind. Remembering you don't *have* to but you *get* to be present for what's happening allows you to prioritize what is important and make the best of your time, no matter what.

FIND THREE THINGS

Take the time to sit down and think of three things you are grateful for. They can be as simple as a good cup of coffee or as profound as the support you received from a friend. Write them down, taking a moment with each to explore that feeling of gratitude. Why is this something you're grateful for? Repeat as often as you'd like! You can make this a monthly, weekly, or even daily practice.

Gratitude is the antidote to overwhelm.

Call It Quits

Can we be real, bestie? We think it's time for you to break up with stress. It's a pretty toxic relationship, and as your friends, we feel like it's time for you to call it quits. You must be tired of the constant push and pull. Stress has made you believe you aren't productive unless you feel overwhelmed. It has been manipulating your emotions and making you question your worth. Stress keeps your thoughts occupied so that you don't truly get a chance to enjoy life. It's time to break up. It's not you, it's stress.

They say that breaking up is hard to do, but we believe in you. You can choose to consciously uncouple and discover who you are when you're not constantly anxious or worried. When you decide to make this change, you'll find it's much easier to stay in the moment, to enjoy the things that are happening around you *while* they happen, rather than worrying about them *before* they do.

Tell your racing thoughts, your anxiety, and your stress, "It's not me, it's you," and kick them to the curb.

WRITE THE BREAKUP LETTER

Write a breakup letter addressed to your stress. Tell it all the ways it has caused you trouble, and explain why it's time to end this toxic relationship. Tell it you've found something new, something that encourages you to live in the moment and accept yourself for who you are, not for what you can do: mindfulness. Describe the life you're going to have, now that you've decided to dump stress and start anew. (Hint: It's going to be awesome.*)*

I am free and separate from my stress.

Make a Mental Map

We're very used to our phones acting as our personal GPS, guiding us from place to place with ease. We have so much trust in them! Not to sound like a total dad, but what would you do if your phone stopped working mid-trip? Gone are the days of keeping an atlas in your car just in case. Instead, you'd have to rely on your knowledge of the area and the mental map you have in your head.

When you're going through life, there are times when your personal GPS goes on the fritz. You know these moments when you see them. They're typically accompanied by the phrases "I don't know why I did that," "I don't know what I'm doing," and "I don't know where to go from here."

In these moments, your responsibilities are simple: Pause to analyze the situation, refer to your internal GPS, and put one foot in front of the other. Before you start the journey, think to yourself, *Where do I want to go and why?* Then map out a course in front of you that you can take little by little.

I can take it one step at a time.

FOLLOW YOUR FEET

Have you ever truly paid attention to the sensation of walking? Now's the time. Take a few quick steps (preferably barefoot so that you can really feel your feet on the ground). Then repeat the process, slowing your steps. Keep doing this until you're moving in borderline slow motion, feeling the sensation of your feet carrying the weight of your body, the way you roll from heel to toe. Don't judge yourself or your movements. Instead, ground yourself (literally) and stay in the present.

Add It to the Calendar

When something is important to you—a birthday, a dinner with a friend, a work meeting—you don't just trust that you'll remember when those things will happen. You add that event's date and time to your calendar. When you're feeling burned-out or stressed, taking a couple seconds to do this feels even more necessary. Because when you're struggling to keep on top of your daily tasks, there's very little chance you'll remember that your aunt Lisa's retirement party is next month.

A calendar is also a visual reminder of the boundaries you have (and have *not*) set with the people in your life. You know the difference between looking at a calendar full of things you're happy to do and one that's full of events and obligations you should've said no to. Adding smaller obligations to your calendar and schedule is a way of alerting yourself to what matters most to you.

There is no shame in reminding yourself to take a few minutes to reconnect with your breath, explore your body, or clear your mind. Mindfulness in any form, for any length of time, is mindfulness. Will you pencil it in?

MINDFUL REMINDERS

It would be nice to be mindful without needing a reminder, but while we're still working our way up to daily practice, there's no shame in physically scheduling in time. Add a calendar reminder or alarm to your phone (or if electronics aren't your thing, your physical calendar or planner) to take five minutes out of your day to practice one of the activities you've learned so far, bringing yourself back to the present.

I can build in time to be mindful.

Surprise and Delight

When a four-year-old says, "This is the best day ever!" they are telling the truth. Well, the truth as *they* see it. Out of their four years on Earth, it probably is their best day . . . yet. That kid is eager to see the awesomeness around them, and they don't feel guilty about ranking this day above others. They're living in the moment, experiencing something new, and everything is a surprise and a delight.

While every day can't be the best day ever, there's something to be said for capturing that feeling of childlike wonder and using it to ground yourself. Though you've lived more years than a four-year-old and experienced the not-always-so-fun realities of life, there is always wonder and joy just around the corner. It's time to get curious about where it could be hiding and make yourself open to receiving it.

When you go through the world with a gentle sense of curiosity, you'll see that you still have so much to learn. Give yourself the time and space to acknowledge and explore the things that bring you joy. The smallest moments can mean something big, if you let them.

WHAT'S NEW?

Sit down at the end of the day (glass of wine or mug of tea optional, but journal encouraged) and write down something new you learned. Slow down, review your day, and think, Did I learn something about myself and the way I react to the world? Did I read something in a book or hear something in a movie or during a conversation with a friend that sparked a feeling in me? *What surprised and delighted you today?*

I learn something new every day.

Connect the Dots

Do you remember when it became popular to use acronyms for everything? LOL, OMG, BRB, ILY. Why take the time to type or say something spelled out when there's a readily available shorthand? There are acronyms to describe the fear of missing out (FOMO) or the fact that you only live once (YOLO). The call to live a nonstop, do-more-or-else existence is ever-present. Unfortunately, TADBATAB (Take a Deep Breath and Take a Break) or SWYT (Sit with Your Thoughts) haven't taken off quite yet.

When you're feeling stressed or anxious, your brain might be trying to connect the dots with either too much or too little data. This is not your fault, but there are ways to see the big picture more clearly.

The great news is our brains have become adept at connecting the dots and gathering data to form opinions and ideas (partially thanks to social media and its love for acronyms). When you choose to take a break from your stress to acknowledge the reality of the situation, you give yourself a chance to gather data and then address it with all of the facts.

S.L.L.

When you feel stressed, overwhelmed, or burned-out, here's a new acronym to try: SLL (Stop, Look, and Listen). Stop: Physically stop what you're doing and take a pause. Look: Identify what's going on around you and what's causing you to feel stressed or anxious. Listen: Pay attention to your body, and listen for what you need next. Do you need a snack? Water? A walk around the block to clear your head? You know what you need; you just need to take a sec to check in with yourself.

I will stop, look, and listen when I feel overwhelmed.

Be Present

We often describe a lack of focus with phrases like: "Your mind wanders." "Your head's not in it." "Your thoughts are elsewhere." These phrases give your mind its own personality—one that cannot stay in the moment, no matter how much you wish it would. You may be sitting in a meeting or driving your car, but your mind is not there with you.

When you feel anxious or overwhelmed and your mind starts wandering off or pushing forward, remind yourself of this simple truth: There is no way to be two places at once. (Unless your boyfriend just drove you to the state line so you can have one foot in each state . . . but we're pretty sure that only happens in early-aughts rom-coms.)

There is only one option: Be wholly where you are. Right now. Right here.

You can make the intentional choice to commit to the moment. Return to your surroundings, even if they aren't perfect or they're a little uncomfortable. Take a deep breath and look around you. Come to your senses. Comfort your tired mind with the truth of this moment.

I AM, RIGHT HERE

In moments of overwhelm, anxiety, or stress, it's important to make a habit of returning to your breath. Your body needs physical and mental reassurance that you're going to be just fine (and trust us: You are going to be just fine). Take a breath in, thinking the words I am, *and then exhale, thinking the words* right here. *Repeat as needed, creating a steady breathing pattern and focusing on where you are right now.*

I am right here, in this very moment.

Find Your Way

Imagine you're walking through a forest, when suddenly you look around and realize the trail markers are nowhere to be seen. At some point, you veered off the path, and now you're lost. As you do your best to retrace your steps and rejoin the trail, the unkempt undergrowth obscures the ground and snags at your pants. Every step feels more perilous than the last. Instead of confidently marching down the path, you are stumbling and frightened.

It doesn't matter how often you've walked the same path, or how confident you were when you set out; dealing with stress and anxiety can leave you feeling aimless, afraid, and lost. Suddenly, what you wanted is out of reach, impossible, and unachievable.

Remember that you have the power to find your way back to the path. You can do this by using mindfulness techniques that connect you to the present and keep you grounded.

You don't need to stumble along through the forest. You can walk tall, pay attention to your surroundings, and make strong decisions to get yourself back on track.

I can trust the path I am on.

REVISIT YOUR TIMELINE

We each have our own unique path to walk, and it's time for you to remember where you came from and how you got here. Going back as far as you can remember, take the time to put every significant, memorable moment of your life onto a timeline. Look at all you have experienced, the breadth of emotions represented, the places you've seen and people you've met that have led up to this very moment. Remember you are exactly where you are supposed to be.

Take It All In

When a racehorse is competing, sometimes it will wear blinders. Why? The blinders limit the horse's field of vision to *only* what's in front of it, in theory allowing the horse to focus on getting to the finish line distraction-free.

You're not a racehorse (as far as we know), but in times of stress and overwhelm, you may feel like you've got racing blinders on. We get it! Everything around you is signaling that slowing down and taking in the world around you would be detrimental to progressing toward your goal. Instead, you're encouraged to speed up and avoid getting distracted so you can win an imaginary race.

Hear us say this: You deserve to see the richness that life brings when you aren't speeding through in the name of productivity. Rather than putting your blinders on, what would happen if you gave yourself permission to take in the world around you? In a day and age where moving swiftly and efficiently is the expectation, slowing down helps you become more mindful of your surroundings and appreciative of the moment you're in.

REMOVE YOUR BLINDERS

This week, when you feel stressed or overwhelmed, set a timer for two minutes and pause. Now take in your space with fresh senses, rather than tunnel vision. What do you see? What do you smell? What do you hear? You may find it hard to break your focus (it may even feel wrong and unproductive). But take two minutes to absorb your surroundings and remind yourself there is so much more to every moment.

I can take in every moment.

Organize Your Thoughts

Some days, your brain feels perfectly organized, bright, and beautiful (like the finished product on a house-flipping show). Other days, it feels like a raccoon came in, found where you were hiding all the clutter, and threw it all over the room. Your thoughts feel scattered, and collecting them becomes a chore. In those moments, you might wonder, *Can I even do this?*

Mindfulness is not some mythical place you enter and stay forever. It is a constant practice of returning to yourself. Some days, you will crush the whole "clear your mind" thing in one try, and other days, your little mind-raccoon will run amok. You'll need to practice organizing your thoughts before you are able to focus.

But you know what? Needing to sit with your thoughts and make sense of them does not mean you are incapable of being mindful. Because being mindful isn't the absence of any thoughts at all—it's the act of meeting your thoughts *without* judgment and *with* curiosity, kindness, and compassion.

Now somebody get that raccoon out of here.

IT'S TIME TO CATEGORIZE

Do you remember playing "categories" as a kid and trying to name the most things in a certain category with your pals? Today, when you're feeling disconnected from the world, stressed out, or overwhelmed, play a one-person game of categories. (Or a multi-person game, if you have a buddy nearby who's willing to join in!) Choose a category and try to name everything you can think of that belongs in it. Focus on one category at a time (dog breeds, for example) and really dedicate yourself to naming an exhaustive list.

I can take my time and sort my thoughts.

DAY 32

Release and Rejoice

Sometimes the act of letting go feels easy, and other times it feels incredibly hard. Sometimes, you open your hand and release what's causing you stress without a fight. Other times, by the time you decide to let go, whatever you were holding is crushed to bits because you've been squeezing it. But remember, you're the one who decides what you're holding and how to hold it. So go ahead and choose to rejoice in the release.

Letting go of stress and anxiety can feel difficult, even when you know that they aren't serving you. Sitting in your stress can feel more comfortable than sitting in stillness and letting your problems work themselves out. Wanting to be in control is so natural.

But when you let go of something that isn't yours to hold, you free up space in your mind to focus on yourself and how you feel. Instead of devoting energy to holding onto control, you get to redirect that energy toward joy and gratitude. You can make the choice to live in the moment.

WRITE IT OUT

Rather than holding all of your emotions and experiences inside and allowing them to pull you from the moment, try this: Take a few minutes to write out everything in your head, either after waking up in the morning or before bed in the evening. You can share your hopes for the day or your worries and fears. As we've learned (and will continue to learn), it's important not to spend your time judging or reflecting on your emotions. Instead, simply let them flow out of you and onto the page, where they'll be until you return.

I do not need to hold on to every thought.

Mindful in the Mundane

Our world is always moving and encouraging us to move along with it. We scroll through social media for hours at a time, buy new gadgets and clothes as trends come and go, and pack our schedules so we can post our experiences for our followers to see.

But what about the moments when everything is quiet? The moments when we aren't paying attention to how quickly the world is turning. Be honest: Do those moments feel unproductive? Do you immediately start to think about everything you should be getting done? Maybe you start planning your meals for the week, your outfit for the next day, or the birthday gift you need to order for your friend.

It's time to embrace the mundane. The next time you find yourself taking it easy or doing a "boring" task, take a moment to remember that there is meaning in everything you do. When you're mindful, you can drop into the present moment and experience life in all its richness by focusing on the details that make it so special and interesting.

I can make anything interesting.

MAKE IT INTERESTING

Next time you are doing a mundane task like washing the dishes, challenge yourself to slow down and truly think through each of your actions. What does the water feel like on your skin? How hot or cold is it? What do the bubbles feel like? How hard are you scrubbing? Focus completely and totally on the task at hand, rather than letting your mind wander. Remain curious and present.

Keep Your Sleep Sacred

We've all been there: scrolling and scrolling before going to sleep (usually way past your self-appointed bedtime) and then waking up and immediately checking your email or scrolling some more.

It's not your fault: Our devices are made to keep us entertained and engaged. You love your phone because you think it makes you connected to what's going on around you, but it's actually doing the opposite. Spending all your free time on your device is making you *less* aware, *less* productive, and *less* happy.

The next time you're lying in bed, pay attention to the way you use your phone. What apps do you reach for? How long do you spend on them? Do you have a pattern of checking one app after another? Are you up late because someone keeps sending you memes? Don't judge yourself for any of your actions. Just note them.

Now try this: Choose to make your bedtime and wake-up routines more mindful by turning your bed into a no-phone zone. You don't have to give up scrolling entirely. Just create a boundary for yourself. Create space to focus on *you* and not your phone.

NO-PHONE ZONE

Give your phone a new place to "sleep"! This shouldn't be anywhere near your bed, which means it might be time for a traditional alarm clock (sorry). Make a point of bringing your charger to your phone's new home, and make the choice to leave your phone in this area when you're ready for bed. This habit encourages you to be present in your bedtime and wake-up routines, eliminating distractions and giving you the chance to listen to your own thoughts rather than drowning them out with endless scrolling. You can do it!

Boundaries help me stay in the moment.

You've Got Dreams

When you were asked what you wanted to be when you grew up, back when you truly believed you could be anything you wanted, what did you say? Were you going to be a ballerina? An astronaut? Some combination of the two?

Whether you realize it or not, you've always had a vision of what you wanted your life to look like. That vision is, of course, ever-changing and evolving with you, but the point is: You know how to dream.

You may not have managed to perform *Swan Lake* on Mars (well, not yet . . .), but one thing is for certain: The life you have right now is full of things you wished for. Take stock of your favorite parts of your life. We bet, at some point or another, recently or long ago, you dreamed of them.

You can use your talent for dreaming to visualize a world where you don't feel run-down, exhausted, stressed, or worried. And what a beautiful dream to dream for yourself, friend. Once you've had the chance to imagine this kind of life for yourself, you can set about making it true.

VISUALIZE A DIFFERENT YOU

Whether you feel like you're perpetually anxious or stressed, or just having one of those days, take a step back and daydream. Visualize a version of you who can stay in the present without allowing their mind to race. How do they carry themselves? What do they feel? Breathe deeply and remember: That is you. Embrace them. Then consider what you need to become them. What tangible steps can you take today?

I can make my visualizations reality.

The Soundtrack of Your Life

Do you ever hear a song that immediately transports you back to an earlier time in your life? The first chord plays, and suddenly you find yourself remembering experiences you may not have thought about in a while, like the freedom of driving in your first car with the windows down, or the giddiness of exploring the mall with your best friend. You may even connect music to some of the serious, emotional times in your life. (Who among us doesn't have a song that immediately brings us to tears?)

Music offers you the opportunity to focus on what you're feeling in the present, even while you're revisiting the past. Some people describe music as an "escape," but what if you used it as means of embracing the moment you're in?

Mindfulness doesn't always need to look like sitting in a dark, quiet room. Life will give you plenty of chances to practice it on the regular. You can sing or dance along and still be practicing mindfulness. Instead of losing yourself in the music, use it to connect to your truth.

I can connect to a specific feeling.

SAY IT IN SONG

It's time to tap into your inner early-aughts rom-com main character. Assign a specific song to what you are feeling and experiencing throughout the day. What song fits the vibe of your morning routine? How about that big meeting you have? What's playing while you're journaling with a cup of coffee? After choosing a song, take a few minutes to listen to it. Focus on how it makes you feel and why it's the perfect score for the present moment, grounding yourself in the now.

Make Your Move

When you're burned-out or overwhelmed, the last thing you want to do is leave the house to work out. We wish we could tell you that moving your body *doesn't* make you feel better so that you could go back to the couch and binge-watch another episode of whatever's on right now, but that would be a lie.

Moving your body, whether that's during an at-home workout, a jog through the park, or a swim at the community gym, does wonders for not just your physical health but also for your mental health. Moving also happens to be a great way to practice mindfulness and build it into your routine.

Think about your favorite form of activity. Do you ever find yourself thinking about everything else you have going on instead of relishing the sensation of movement? You're going on a run, but on the inside, you're taking your mind off the activity by listening to a true crime podcast or planning carpool schedules for the week. See what happens when you sync up your mind and body, when you focus on what your body is doing right now in this moment.

WORK IT OUT

Whatever your preferred workout or form of movement, take time today to do it mindfully. As you're completing the exercise, think about the way your muscles tense and bunch and how they feel when they're at rest. Feel the sweat on your skin and the fabric of your clothing against your body. You can even do this when you're simply walking from your desk to the printer at work. Really pay attention as you move, focusing solely on the movement you are performing.

I can move mindfully and with intention.

Capable and in Control

Bestie, has that voice inside your head been telling you that you aren't good enough again? Imposter syndrome is so real, and it rears its ugly head when you're feeling at your lowest. It's like the person who says, "That looks heavy," instead of offering to help carry whatever you're struggling to hold. Not helpful!

Luckily, that voice inside your head belongs to someone you know very well: *you*. You have the final say in whether or not you believe anything it says. You get to correct the record. That can be difficult to do when you're feeling stressed or anxious, because lies are easier to believe when you've dropped a ball or two, are extremely tired, or are feeling burned-out.

There will be days when you simply do not have it in you to fight, and these are the kinds of days we plan for. Like a person preparing frozen meals before a big surgery so they have something easy and delicious to heat up, you can store up your confidence in a way that allows you to access it later—when you need it most.

THE "I CAN DO THIS" LIST

Write out a list of small actions you can do in moments of stress or overwhelm. These should be actions you already know help you feel better, like taking a walk, calling a friend, having a snack (being hangry doesn't help anything!), or pausing to take a few deep breaths. Consider this your mindfulness arsenal. You can pull from this list any time you want to come back to the present. You can also build on it throughout this journey. Refer back to it as often as you need.

I have the tools I need to stay mindful.

Don't Fall for Clickbait

No matter where you're consuming your news lately (even if it's just on social media), there's no denying the power of a headline. The headline is meant to grab your clicks, tell the broadest version of the story, and ultimately make you read the entire article.

In your own life, you are both reporter and subject, telling yourself what to think and feel about the things you experience. Unfortunately, these days, your stress and anxiety have you reporting inaccurately; they're telling you lies rather than reporting the objective truth. For example, your stress would report, *Boss Asks Employee to "Meet ASAP," Firing Imminent.* But what happens if you try to report the truth? Suddenly the story is *Boss Asks Employee to Meet, Which Is Part of Having a Job.*

We want to be clear: This is not an excuse to push down your emotions or ignore them altogether. The hope is that, when you break down the day into the Good, Bad, or Neutral, you have the opportunity to view everything from an objective, judgment-free zone.

I can find things to celebrate.

SHARE THE HIGHLIGHTS

Extra, extra! Read all about it! In the headlines-only version of your day, the one where all the fluff is cut, what were the top stories? Whether they were big moments like "Dedicated Employee Gets Promotion!" or smaller ones like "Local Student Pets Two Dogs on the Way to Class," find the most significant parts of your day, and make them front-page news. Don't shy away from any of your emotions or experiences. Simply reflect on them and record the headlines in your journal.

Manage Your To-Do List

How do you feel about to-do lists? Everyone has their preference. Some are pen-and-paper traditionalists, some have reminders in their phone, some are living (*gasp*) *without* a to-do list.

If you're someone who has gotten caught up in their to-do list, you're not alone. For a while there, everyone was saying, "You have the same number of hours in a day as Beyoncé," but we'll be honest with you: Beyoncé has many, *many* people tackling her to-do list. If you try to do life like Beyoncé, you will burn out. So why the heck is *your* to-do list—the one you do all by yourself—always a mile long?

We're not suggesting you do away with your list entirely (we're not monsters). Rather, we'd like you to rethink the way you use it. Instead of letting your list overwhelm you and send you into a spiral as you take in *all* the things you need to accomplish at once, we'd like to use it as a focus tool that allows you to get stuff done, one task at a time.

BREAK IT DOWN

You're going to make a to-do list. But here's the catch: You can only write down one item on it at a time. Start small, devoting your time and energy to that singular task. When you're done, cross off the task and then add your next one. This keeps you focused on the present, rather than spiraling when you see how much you need to do and attempting to skip ahead. (Pro tip: If you've already got a full list written down, cover all but one task with a sticky note instead.)

My life is so much bigger than a list.

Fun and Games

Playtime—the hours you spend imagining, creating, building (and knocking down) with friends and on your own—is a huge part of your formative early years. There are plenty of reasons that playing is important: It's how you learn to exercise creativity and curiosity while learning to share, problem solve, and express emotion.

At some point, you stopped playing so much. We don't blame you! Adulting is hard, and life gets busy. There's less time and more responsibility. By the time you finish the day, you're exhausted from carrying it all. Playing doesn't even make it into the Top 25 of things you want or need to do when you get home.

It may seem silly, bestie, but it's time to make playing a priority, especially while you look to enter a new, more mindful era of your life. Playing gives you the chance to focus on what you're touching, seeing, hearing, and feeling. It requires attention and intention, and yes, you even get to have some fun. It's time that *you* get to choose what brings you joy and commit to doing it. Wanna play?

SCHEDULE A PLAYDATE

Okay, okay, scheduling "fun" may sound like the exact opposite, but when you're overwhelmed and overscheduled, you'll need to practice carving out time for play and whimsy before it becomes second nature. Grab your planner or calendar and schedule a playdate for yourself this week. You can block out fifteen minutes or three hours, as long as you're scheduling time to do something that connects you to your childlike wonder and creativity. Find your favorite game, activity, or arts and crafts project from childhood and have fun.

I can reconnect with my sense of wonder through play.

Clear Your Mind

Being burned-out feels a lot like trying to do your hair in front of a foggy mirror. Sure, you can see the outline of yourself, and maybe there's even a moment where you can wipe away some of the condensation to catch a glimpse of your reflection, but you cannot see clearly. Your hair *might* turn out all right despite the circumstances, but it won't be anywhere near your best. The people around you may tell you it looks amazing, all things considered, but their praise just won't mean much when you know you could've done better.

It's time to defog your mirror and allow yourself to see clearly. When you give yourself the time and space to clear your mind, you give yourself permission to fill your head with all the good things around you. When you wash away the pain of rejection, you can see opportunity. When you get rid of frustration, you can see what needs fixing. When you remove bitterness, you can see gratitude. You deserve to see the world clearly, apart from the stress and anxiety you're feeling.

WIPE IT AWAY

When your thoughts are racing, close your eyes and imagine them like raindrops hitting the windshield of your car. Don't judge how hard it's raining or what thoughts come up. Simply let them come and go. When you're ready, imagine turning on the windshield wipers and removing every raindrop from the windshield. Wipe the windshield of your mind clean, so that you can return to the present moment with a clear head.

I can clear my mind to focus on the moment.

Give Yourself a Hand

Taking a tumble is never fun. The feeling of falling without being able to control how you land and knowing that you're probably going to walk away with a few bumps and bruises is, well, scary.

There are plenty of things that trip us up and leave us with a skinned knee or two. Right now, the thing pushing you over might be stress or anxiety. Often, those feelings don't just knock you over. Sometimes, they can keep you on the ground and make you feel like getting up isn't worth the effort. Why go through the ordeal of getting to your feet if you're just going to end up on your back again anyway?

Life is made up of spills and falls. They teach us to learn from our mistakes and get back up again. Mindfulness is the hand reaching out to you, ready to pull you up so you can dust yourself off and try again.

When you feel yourself falling, or if you're already down for the count, don't jump to judging yourself. Instead, reach out a hand and find an invitation to mindfulness waiting for you.

HIGH FIVE

Hold your hand out in front of you. Using your forefinger on your opposite hand, trace your fingers (sort of like you would if you were tracing them onto a piece of paper). Breathe in as you travel up to the tip of each finger, and then breathe out as you head down the other side. Do this a few times, back and forth along the hand, paying attention to the sensations of your fingers and visualizing your breath.

I can find my breath and choose to try again.

Be on the Lookout

Life is a big game of hide-and-seek. And you, my friend, are the seeker. Right now, the things that bring you joy and connection are all hidden behind stress, anxiety, overwork, and burnout.

The good news is, you know *all* the best hideouts, and you're determined to find every last one, rather than giving up and yelling "olly olly oxen free" (not that you've ever really understood why we yell that anyway when the game is done).

When you're practicing mindfulness, you give your brain the chance to disengage from your stress spiral for long enough to return to the present moment. You do this by being an expert seeker.

Drop into the moment and look around you. Notice what you can see in the space around you. Delight in the things you find, both big and small. In those moments, you're able to be on the lookout for the positive things in your life that bring you joy and happiness, which are the things you should focus on.

Go ahead—no need to count to one hundred before you start looking. You've got this.

TAKE A WALK

This sounds too simple to be true, but coming back to your body and mind can be achieved by simply taking a walk. You don't need to trek for miles—around the block counts! Don't let your worries follow you out the door. Rather than focusing on mistakes you made or things you need to do, spend your walk narrating what you see. Get granular: Describe the way your surroundings look, smell, sound, and feel. Find beauty in your world.

I can take in the beauty of my surroundings.

Gold Star

Remember being a kid and getting a gold star sticker from your teacher for any behavior they wanted to reinforce? You get a sticker! And *you* get a sticker! Everybody gets a sticker! It was both a reward and a tangible way to signal a job well done (even if that job was just being line leader that morning). It gave you something to hold up and hold on to.

Somewhere along the way, the universe decided that adults didn't get gold stars or prizes (and to borrow a word from elementary school, we think that's bogus). Instead, when we finish a task, we simply move on to the next one without anything to mark our success or accomplishment.

Now that you're an adult, *you* have to be the one to celebrate yourself. We challenge you to celebrate everything, big or small, by pausing, stepping away, and treating yourself. And a "treat yourself" moment goes further than just material goods. You can treat yourself with kindness or words of affirmation. If you can't make time for your favorite little treat, at least make time to pat yourself on the back and compliment yourself.

I can practice self-care.

TREAT YOURSELF

Sometimes self-care can feel more like a chore than a treat. Who has time to go to the salon and finally get that much-needed cut-and-color? You deserve a little treat for making it through that meeting, that dentist appointment, or that workout class. Make time today to celebrate victories big and small by treating yourself. This could be your favorite coffee, a new book, a delicious meal, or a lavish bubble bath. Whatever makes you feel appreciated and accomplished works!

I can look back and appreciate where I've come from.

I can look forward with enthusiasm for where I am going.

Get a Good Start

Whether or not you're a morning person, the first moments of your day set the tone for what follows. If the fairy-tale princesses of your youth are to be believed, it's possible to wake up, have a big yawn and stretch, look as flawless as you did the night before (despite not washing your face before bed), and begin your day with the energy of someone who has woodland creatures sweeping the floor.

But when your alarm doesn't go off and your coffee machine is on the fritz and your favorite shirt is in the wash, chances are the frenetic, chaotic energy of your morning will follow you into your day.

You may have heard something about the importance of starting how you intend to finish. It's not about *how* you finish; it's about your *intention* to do so. When you're mindful about the beginning of the day, you can train your brain to return to that mindful state later. If you spend the first moments of your morning actively setting a positive intention for the day, you're better prepared to come back to that periodically throughout the day.

SET YOUR INTENTION

Before you start running around with the hustle and bustle of your daily schedule, take a moment to set your intention for the day. Write it down and return to it whenever you feel out of control. Some examples might be: I will choose positivity and joy. I can do difficult things. I embrace growth and change. *Repeat your intention to yourself as you move through your day, using it as something to focus on—especially when the day is difficult.*

I can approach each day with a clear intention.

Surround Sounds

Tell us if this scenario sounds familiar: It's hot, your bag is slipping off your shoulder, your jeans fit weird today, and it's *loud*. It's loud not just in your head, but all around you. You're overstimulated, bestie. People (and pets) are constantly asking you for something, calling your name, and tugging on your sleeve, and you're doing your best to juggle it all.

Something tells us that "juggling it all" isn't working. In fact, it's pulling you further and further away from being able to live in the moment and find enjoyment in your life. The answer to this problem is turning down the volume of your life. It's time to mute the unhelpful noise holding you back.

As backward as it may sound, listening and hearing with intention is an important part of the muting process (and of mindfulness as a whole). When you focus on one sound at a time, you teach your brain to focus and return to (and enjoy!) the task at hand. You also fight overstimulation, as intentional listening allows you to hear that little voice in your head above the din.

There is so much to hear; I'm ready to listen.

SELECTIVE HEARING

Take a seat somewhere comfortable and close your eyes. Listen for a sound—this can be the air conditioner blowing, the sound of a car driving by, or a conversation happening a few feet away. Even though there may be more sounds happening around you, focus on that one sound. How loud or soft is it? Does its tone change? How long does the sound last? Focus your mind, and seek to hear on a whole new level.

In the Waiting

Whether we're waiting for a bus that was scheduled to arrive fifteen minutes ago, a promotion at work that is overdue, or a microwave meal that's going to take five minutes—we have all at some time or another been waiting for something we wanted right this minute.

We live in a world of instant gratification. When you forget something, you have it delivered via app. You see a sweater on an influencer, and you click Add to Cart. You don't order something if you can't get it with two-day shipping.

Suddenly, you're not waiting for something good to happen, you're becoming restless and agitated that it's not happening *right this instant*. Then, as your mind wanders, you start planning for the future and its many possibilities, and opportunities to jump to the worst-case scenario are plentiful.

It is so important that you practice waiting well. And "waiting well" means you focus on what you want and why it's worth the wait. It means you do not gloss over these moments of waiting that make "the getting" all the sweeter. Instead, choose to savor the wait.

LET YOURSELF LINGER

Embrace the practice of lingering: staying in the place where you are or the situation you're in for longer than necessary. This might feel uncomfortable at first, but instead of running off to your next appointment or tackling another task, linger in the moment. Use all of your senses to take everything in. You won't get the same moment twice, so treat it like the gift it is (no take- backs!) and take your time with it.

I can linger and appreciate the moment at hand.

Look Through a New Lens

The beauty of spending time with small children is that they're never embarrassed to be amazed by the mundane, to ask the questions, to let wonder show plainly on their faces. Something as simple as a paper towel dispenser in a gas station bathroom provides them with surprise and delight. The light reflecting off of someone's watch and onto the wall becomes magical and dazzling. Water bubbling out of a fountain is wondrously baffling.

Each gleeful shout of "Look!" from a little kid (or even an ears-perked head tilt from a furry friend) is an invitation to join them in the present moment. You get so busy speeding through your day, your mind constantly charging ahead to the next thing on your list, that it's easy to miss out on the specialness of right now.

Remember, you don't need to wait for the next time you're around babies and puppies to look at your world in a new, sparkly light. Everything they notice is there for you to see too. You just need to slow down, open your eyes, shake off any self-consciousness, and see the wonder.

FIND THE FACES

One of the most whimsical quirks of our humanity is that our brains are programmed to see faces everywhere. There's the house down the street that looks like it has rectangular eyes (its windows) and a gaping mouth (the garage) and the bolts on the ceiling fan that lend eyes to the curved blade's smile. We usually see these "faces" without trying. Take notice today. Pay attention to which faces look happy, sad, or silly. Think about the imaginary personalities and feelings of the faces on the signs, sidewalks, and cabinets you encounter.

I can find the magic in the everyday.

Take a Moment

Real talk: No matter how busy you are—and we're not doubting you're busy—you have sixty seconds to spare for yourself. You may not feel like that's true, with all the appointments and the meetings and the housework on your plate. But we promise you'll find that extra minute if you look for it.

When you give yourself permission to pause, you'll find that you are clearer-headed and more understanding of your own needs—and the needs of others. Pausing can help you feel compassion for those who don't know how to do so themselves (and, as a result, are making your life more stressful).

It's time to face the facts: The world will *not* spin off its axis if you even think about taking a break. The truth is, nothing detrimental will happen if you take a break to reconnect with yourself. You can put down your phone, close out your email, and allow yourself to take a moment to explore your senses. This break will give you the opportunity to focus on yourself and your body without distraction.

I deserve a moment to reconnect.

MINUTE TO WIN IT

Set a timer for a minute and then . . . take that minute. Take what you need to ground yourself in that minute. Seriously, taking a break is that simple. Close your eyes and breathe deeply, in and out. During this time, you can focus on your breath or use your senses to connect to the space around you (what you see, hear, touch, taste, or smell). Don't rush. Simply sit for one minute and reset. Then come back to your present moment.

The Good-Enough Now

We hope we're not the first to tell you (that would be awkward), but you're not perfect. We know, we know. The world would have you believe perfection is not only possible, but that you're just *one* step away from it at all times.

This belief only keeps you striving. You want to get as close to perfection as possible, but where has that gotten you? Stressed, burned-out, worrying over things that have not even happened yet, and struggling to stay connected to the people, places, and activities you love.

When you accept that you'll never attain perfection, you unlock a compassion for yourself that allows you to believe that, while you're not perfect, you *are* awesomely complicated. Friend, everyone has bad days and makes mistakes. When you accept this and learn to let go of perfection in favor of "good enough," you end a vicious cycle and reconnect to the things that bring you the most joy.

When there isn't so much noise distracting you, you can focus on the moment you're in and all the reasons you're grateful for it—in all its perfectly imperfect glory.

LET IT PASS

Imagine you're sitting in a field on a beautiful spring day. Birds, bees, butterflies, and bunnies are constantly coming and going. Label each critter with an emotion you're feeling or a worry you're having. Acknowledge them as they come, and then allow your concerns to flit, fly, or hop away with the creatures who stopped by for a visit. You can acknowledge your feelings without allowing them to overwhelm you.

I can find peace in what's happening right now.

Let's Get Fancy

There are probably "fancy" things you keep in your house for special occasions. Your grandma's dinnerware that only gets used on major holidays, an expensive scent you only wear to important events, or the outfit in the back of your closet that you're saving for some future occasion. Heck, you even do this with your favorite drinks and snacks, dragging out the experience of consuming them over as many days as possible.

This is a scarcity mindset. You're afraid to use your most precious, special things because you want to preserve and reserve them for some undetermined someday. But we hate to break it to you: This is just another way to escape to the future, rather than focusing on right now.

Instead of imagining when you'll be able to use these things *someday* and keeping them untouched on your highest shelf, allow yourself to commit to this very moment. It is, after all, the only one that is promised to you. How can you embrace the importance of these objects while still allowing yourself to experience them? Give yourself permission to make the ordinary feel exceptional.

USE THE BEST

Today is your special occasion. Make the decision to use whatever you've been saving for "someday" today. Use the expensive lotion, throw on those gorgeous shoes you'd feel weird wearing to the grocery store, make your favorite food, or eat the fancy chocolate. We are only promised this very moment, so revel in the joy of treating yourself to the things you once decided were too nice or too fancy. Don't pass judgment on yourself for deciding to treat yourself. Focus on accepting these things with joy and gratitude.

Every day is a special occasion. I will enjoy today.

Commit to Your Commute

Your life is full of commutes: short walks to the refrigerator, long walks to your friend's place, a thirty-minute drive to work, an hour to visit family. Whether you get to and from your destination in a car or on a plane, train, boat, or your own two feet, you are commuting.

Often, your mind is thinking ahead to where you're going: what you'll do when you get there, who you'll see, and how you'll feel. You stress over logistics; you plan every step. You hate to be late or (even worse) hit traffic, which makes the destination you're focused on feel farther away. Even when you are mid-commute, your mind isn't on the road, it's on the future.

Challenge yourself to focus on each step of your journey as you take it, rather than fixating on the destination. Each step forward is a step toward where you're meant to be, and you're allowed to enjoy every one of them. We're not saying you suddenly need to *love* sitting in traffic, but remember, the destination will always be there. Slow down, friend. Enjoy the journey.

GET THERE, STEP-BY-STEP

Add mindfulness into your commute, focusing on the moment you're in and not on the destination you're headed, or anything that needs to be done when you get there. Break down your commute step by step. For example, focus on the simple act of locking your front door before thinking about the traffic you may face. When you focus on one step at a time, you can remain grounded in the present and keep your mind from racing ahead to whatever you have on your schedule.

I can enjoy each step of the journey.

Attention, Please!

Mindfulness is all about observing. To be mindful is to be constantly noticing *when* you need to be mindful and then using your senses to do so.

You notice your mind is racing, so you pause and take a breath. You realize you need a mindful moment, so you direct your focus to the feeling of the ground beneath your feet, the smell of a candle, the taste of your coffee, or the noises and sights around you. You use these senses to bring you back to yourself.

We can go further. Don't simply return to the moment; celebrate it. So many things in our lives go unnoticed. Take in your surroundings and honor them by seeing what makes them special. The work does not need to stop once you've returned to your senses; it is a continual state of attention.

Become the kind of person who notices what other people don't. Become the kind of person who takes joy in the little things. The world is shouting, "Can I have your attention, please?" Your answer should be a resounding, enthusiastic, "Yes!"

I will notice everything, big and small.

DON'T LET IT GO UNNOTICED

There are many people, places, and things that go unnoticed throughout the day, but this journey to mindfulness is all about noticing them. Today, find five things that typically go unmentioned and unnoticed. The person at work who always replaces the tissue box when it's empty, the dog walker who greets you every day with a smile, the shining sun, or the umbrella you remembered to grab before a storm. Shout your praise from the rooftops, or add them to a list in your phone, but do not let them go unnoticed today!

Take On the Mountain

When you look at a mountain from far away, you may feel that reaching its peak seems impossible. It's too big, too far, too . . . everything. Here's the secret, friend: No one climbs a mountain all at once. You need to take the climb one step at a time.

When you focus on putting one foot in front of the other, you give yourself the opportunity to enjoy the experience instead of dreading the journey before it even starts.

Have you ever neglected doing a task because it seemed like too much to take on? The laundry gets left in the hamper, the dishes pile up, or you put off your passion project for when you "have more time." You tell yourself you'll get to it when you have more energy, or when the need gets to be too big to ignore, only to keep moving the starting line.

It's time to climb the mountain (even if it's one made of laundry). Focus on putting one small task in front of the other, making incremental moves until you reach the summit.

BEAT THE CLOCK

Write down a list of tasks you've been putting off (whether for a few months or a few days). Next to each task, write down how long you think it'll take to do. Then, set a timer and focus. Your job is to beat the clock, bestie. You don't have to do every task today, just pick one. When you're finished, write down the actual time it took you to do that task. The next time it's on your list, you'll remember that you can focus and beat your expectations.

I am capable of meeting and beating my expectations.

DAY 56

Chase the Glimmers

By this point, you've done a fair bit of practicing mindfulness, observing your thoughts without judging them and allowing yourself to focus on the present. Now it's time take it a step further.

When you approach your thoughts and feelings mindfully, you get better at discerning what is true and choosing how you respond. Instead of resisting your feelings, pushing them down, or brushing them off, you accept them for what they are. Once you accept them, you can make a choice to *also* notice the glimmers of good that coexist alongside the less positive thoughts.

This doesn't mean difficulty and negativity will completely disappear from your life, but two things can be true at the same time: You may experience grief, but you can also experience generosity. You may experience betrayal, but you can also experience support. Disappointment may be accompanied by excitement. Can you open your mind to see it all?

You don't need to turn everything into a positive (that would just be unrealistic). But you can make the choice to seek out the good in your circumstances and give yourself more balance.

ON THE PLUS SIDE

Grab your journal and something to write with, and create two columns on a page. The first column is for your unfiltered thoughts—whatever is occupying space in your mind right now. In that column, jot down a list of what is making you feel stressed, worried, anxious, or simply preoccupied. The second column is a space to find the glimmers. You acknowledged the negatives in the first column. Now ask yourself where you can see the light shining through. That's where the magic happens.

I seek and find the glimmers of good.

Feed Your Fire

Even if you've never started a fire on your own before, you've probably watched someone do it in person or on TV. You start by lighting a match and holding it to something small and easy to burn, known as *tinder*. The tinder goes up in flames, catches the kindling, and then that burns for long enough to light larger pieces of wood. *Voilà!* Fire!

You may think that mindfulness is just a small part of your day. But here's the truth: You can't build a full-fledged, self-sustaining fire without the small bits of flammable material. The small, actionable pieces of mindfulness you incorporate into your life now are creating a pattern that will grow and expand into larger areas of your life.

Every time you choose to return to the present moment or pause to regain your awareness of the world around you, you're adding fuel to your fire and meaning to your life. Don't underestimate the power that can be found in a moment of pause or a mindful breath: They are the foundations of a strong blaze.

A GUIDING LIGHT

Find a relatively dark, comfortable place in your home and grab a candle. Place the candle a couple feet away from you and light it. Then watch the flame. Notice how it moves and dances. (If having an open flame around isn't your thing, you can also close your eyes and visualize the flame.) If your mind ends up wandering, no worries! As with other mindfulness exercises, just return to the task at hand and try to stay focused.

My small, mindful steps fuel my life's fire.

Focus on Friendship

What does being a "good" friend mean to you? So much of relationship is give and take. A call and response. Something needed and something given. Many of us know what it's like to be in a one-sided friendship, where one person consumes all the energy and the other gives and gives until they no longer have the capacity.

This is where mindfulness comes in handy.

No relationship is completely fifty-fifty, and no two relationships look the same. However, when you're making an effort to be mindful, your relationships will benefit. As you teach yourself to recognize your thoughts, actions, and feelings, you become more attuned to those of others. You give people more than just your relationship. You give them space to be seen, heard, and understood.

This makes you the best kind of friend—one who listens and learns. One who knows without having to ask, who intuits what the other is feeling and what kind of support they need. You may not be the perfect friend (there's no such thing), but you will be a perfectly present one.

PICK UP THE PHONE

We know, we know: Nobody calls anyone anymore. Well, bestie, you do! Today, pick up the phone, call a friend, and be present. We know it's tempting to multitask while you're on the phone, but do your best to devote your time and energy to listening to your friend. Ask them how they're doing, hear their highs and lows of the days or weeks since you last spoke, and be intentional about what you choose to talk about. You may even end up making this a consistent practice together!

I can devote my energy to people who matter.

Get Creative

When you've got a lot going on, sometimes you may feel that if you're not the best at something (or, for the overachievers reading this, the best at *everything*), you shouldn't even try.

Maybe you feel that even when you *are* great at something, you put so much pressure on having a perfect outcome that what you once loved suddenly feels . . . all wrong. Your mind may tell you that anything less than the best is a waste of time.

When was the last time you let yourself just *be*? No expectations. No pressure.

When you embrace mindfulness and commit yourself to remaining present, the outcome stops being the whole point. You realize the "point" is made up of those little moments in the middle—the ones that remind you that you can enjoy yourself without clinging to perfection.

In these moments, creativity *thrives*, because being creative is not about making the most perfect, beautiful thing in the world; it's about expressing yourself. You are a perfectly imperfect, marvelously messy, immensely interesting person. So settle into yourself, breathe deep, and let yourself make moment-by-moment decisions. Things are bound to get interesting.

I can embrace life's messiness.

MAKE A MESS

Find something that you don't mind ruining, like a cardboard box or magazine you've had for way too long. Now get to work making a mess of it! Grab some scissors, and cut up that box or paper into teeny, tiny pieces. Rip, crumple, fold—whatever you feel like doing. Focus on the sensations you're feeling while you do. Listen to the sounds of your task. What do you feel while you make a bit of a mess? What feelings or thoughts come up? Gently acknowledge them, let them go, and get back to work!

Go with the Flow

Look, we all *want* to be someone who goes with the flow. But since you're working on being mindful and living in the moment, we've got a feeling that your inner monologue sounds a lot less like, *Sure, let's play it by ear,* and more like, *What time does the flow start? Who is going to the flow? Will the flow be fast or slow? Where do I park when I get there?*

Mindfulness is all about trying to quiet that inner monologue, allowing yourself to enjoy life as you experience it. It's okay and totally normal to have these flow-controlling thoughts, but it's important to pick and choose which thoughts are worth your precious time so you don't spend your life worrying.

Your mind *is* the flow. You can either fight against it or allow it to carry you to the next destination. There will always be things (aka *your thoughts*) floating by in the river that you can choose to interact with or let float away. By discerning which are worth disrupting your flow, you learn to enjoy the ride.

RIDE THE RIVER

Close your eyes and take a few deep breaths. Imagine your mind as a flowing river. Does it feel like it's flowing fast, filled with rapids and currents? Or is it a slow-flowing, lazy river, meandering on without hurry? Now imagine your thoughts and concerns are leaves floating down the river. Rather than attempting to pluck the leaves from the moving current and bring them to shore, allow them to pass you by as you focus on the here and now.

I let my thoughts go with the flow.

To Buy or Not to Buy

Many of us are fortunate to live in a world where when we see something we like, we can simply add it to our shopping cart. We don't even need to leave the house.

Impulse buying has become the norm. We don't always think through purchases before making them. When you make the decision to be more mindful, you invite intentionality into every decision, including how you spend your time and money.

Mindfulness encourages you to take an intentional pause, which allows you to consider all scenarios and make an informed decision. This isn't to say you have to avoid shopping altogether, but what would it look like to pause before you whip out your credit card?

You can ask yourself, *Do I really need this, or am I shopping to fill an emotional need? Am I feeling bored, sad, stressed, or lonely? Will I want this in a week? A month? A year?*

If you commit to pausing and checking in with yourself before you click Checkout, you practice the skill of acting thoughtfully rather than impulsively. And that's worth so much more than another cute sweater.

PUT YOUR CART IN TIME-OUT

In your journal or on your phone, create a "time-out" for your shopping cart. Write down the name of the item you think you want and how much it costs. Then commit to a month (or a time frame of your choosing) of not buying that product. Every time you think of the item, you can add it to your time-out list again as a visual reminder that you're practicing intentionality over your Add to Cart impulse. Give your brain some space to think through purchases so you can understand what you want versus what you need.

I can control my impulses and make mindful choices.

Be a Friend to Yourself

Think of the last time you got an unsolicited compliment from someone. How did it make you feel? These unprompted moments of kindness have the power to completely turn your day around—that's how impactful they are.

When was the last time you complimented yourself? It's okay if it's been a while—we are often our own worst critics. Even if you can show kindness to others, there are times when you can't seem to extend that same kindness to yourself. Instead, you see only the ways you're falling short, rather than focusing on your successes, or at least giving yourself grace and trying again.

One way to combat this unfortunate, negative feedback loop in your head is by practicing kindness toward yourself. When we meet ourselves with kindness rather than judgment, we open the door to viewing our experiences in a more objective, positive way.

When you treat yourself with compassion, you're able to live more fully in the moment, and you become more mindful of how you speak to yourself, rather than letting shame or anxiety creep in to steal your joy.

FIVE KIND THINGS

Take a pause to think of five compliments to give yourself today. (Better yet, write them down so you can refer to them next time you're feeling down on yourself!) Try not to make them physical—start by focusing on your personality, the way you treat others, and the things you've done well. When you practice speaking kindly to yourself, you stop the negative narrative in your head before it can be worsened by stress, burnout, anxiety, and overwhelm.

I deserve kindness, especially from myself.

Nobody Puts You in a Corner

Stress, anxiety, and overwhelm can make you feel so small—like you're always *reacting* to people, your surroundings, your long list of to-dos.

You may feel as if you're stuck in a room where you've been relegated to one corner, and there is no space for you to *experience* life. You've made yourself small just to fit semi-comfortably, and now you're going through the (very restricted) motions, unable to express your feelings for fear they won't fit. When you feel like this, you start to resent the people and things around you: They seem like they're *also* taking up your limited square footage.

Friend, it's time to make some space. Start with clearing out the mental clutter: Close your eyes, take a few deep breaths, and connect with your body. Give yourself permission to live in the moment, no matter how messy that moment feels. Open your eyes and survey the room around you. Connect with how you feel, what you need, and what you want to experience. Then step out, ready to experience the space in all its fullness.

TAKE UP SPACE

Practice belly breathing by lying on your back on a flat surface. Put your hands on your stomach. Close your eyes and breathe in. Feel your body fill with air. Imagine sending the air to your belly, and feel the way it rises. Then breathe out, feeling how your belly deflates beneath your palms. Sit with your breath for at least three minutes, paying attention without judgment to the feelings you have as you do.

I can feel my breath making space for me.

Loosen Up

If you practice yoga or any kind of stretching routine, you'll find that, over time, you become more and more flexible. The first time you try to bend over and touch your toes, for example, may not be a success. Your muscles may feel tight, and you might not get anywhere close to your toes.

But with some patience and consistency, you'll find that the more you practice, the looser your muscles will feel, and the easier it becomes to sink into the stretch. Over time, you'll get closer and closer to your fingertips grazing the floor.

Life itself is a constant practice of stretching. You cannot rush it (or you could pull a muscle or hurt yourself). Some experiences feel uncomfortable at first, until you encounter them so often that they become simple. When you're brave enough to try something new, you'll need to repeat the process, working to get it right (or as close to right as you possibly can).

How is life stretching you lately? Where can you take your time and, rather than rushing through the moment, sink intentionally into the stretch?

THE MORNING STRETCH

Every morning this week, make a practice of stretching your body before you start your day. You can even do this from your bed (if you can trust yourself not to fall back to sleep!). Take a few gentle twists, turning your knees to one side and then the other. Do a forward fold while sitting down or standing up. If you're up for it, find a video online of a quick yoga class or stretch session. Feel your body waking up to a brand-new day.

I'm being stretched so I can grow.

Capture Your Peace

"Take a picture, it'll last longer," but make it sincere. Photo albums—physical or digital—aren't just full of memories to reminisce about. They become living, breathing proof of your day-to-day life. They've got everything from pictures of dinner at that one restaurant you loved to screenshots of conversations you needed to share with your bestie.

If you looked through your photo album right now, what would it say about you? Are you someone who takes pictures of anything that strikes your fancy? Or do you get so caught up in the moment that you have to rely on friends to send you photos later? Do you have endless inspo screenshots—for recipes, DIY projects, travel destinations, dates, outfits, and so on? Hopefully there are pockets of peace and joy in your photos too.

Each time you pick up your phone to take a photo is an opportunity to be mindful. You're already pausing to take the picture; now you can commit the details of the moment to memory. How? By slowing down, focusing on what made the moment special enough to record, and capturing a photo of your peace.

I can remember my peace.

SNAPSHOTS OF SERENITY

Throughout your day, take little snapshots of things that bring you joy. Take photos of everything from your morning latte to your child's backpack at the front door to your dog's tail wagging. Don't judge the things that bring you joy. Simply accept them as your due (because you deserve to be happy, bestie!) and move on. When you're feeling overwhelmed or anxious, look back through your camera roll to remind yourself that there is joy to be found in the little things. The peaceful moments are there to fill you.

Get the Deets

Do you have anyone in your life who is *not* detail-oriented? You love them, but they're the kind of person who will tell you something simple like, "Stephanie is throwing a party on Saturday. Come by!" That's it. No follow-up information. One sentence *seems* like the whole story, but really, there are crucial details missing: What time is the party? What are you celebrating? What is the dress code? Is it kid-friendly? Do you need to bring anything?

The lack of detail makes planning or adjusting your expectations difficult. Without those details, you might show up to a fancy dinner party in jeans and a T-shirt, or to a kid's birthday party without your child, or to a potluck without an appetizer.

When you feel overwhelmed or anxious, your brain starts to fill you in on fewer details. In these moments, take some time to return to the present and go on a fact-finding mission. When you focus on the details, one at a time, you slow down your mind and can enjoy the party when you arrive (wearing just the right outfit).

PAY CLOSE ATTENTION

Take time to pause and look around you. Observe the space you're in right now. Are you in a room you recognize well? Or is it a brand-new space? Notice the specific shade of the walls, the texture of the furniture, and the feel of the floor beneath your feet. Pick out ten details that you normally wouldn't notice at first glance. See how granular you can get, pinpointing your sharp senses on the fine details to ground yourself in the space.

I focus on the details to paint a clearer picture.

Drop the Ball

Have you ever watched a circus juggling act? They usually start off pretty tame, with one person juggling a few rubber balls. As the act continues, the juggler incorporates more and more balls. Then they might juggle something more impressive like a bowling pin, or something breakable like a glass plate. The stakes continue to get higher and higher until there's a chainsaw in the mix. We, as the audience, watch intently to see if the juggler will drop something.

Does your life ever feel like this juggling act? Are you afraid you might drop something? Or—worse—that everyone will see when you do? Friend, you're not a trained professional, nor are all eyes on you in the center ring. You don't need to keep everything in the air all the time.

Not everything you're juggling is breakable; you can drop those things and pick them back up again. Others are more fragile—you can't drop those, and we get that. But you can gently *set* them down, step back, and feel the freedom that comes with unburdened arms for a second. You get to choose when to stop and start.

WHAT ARE YOU JUGGLING?

On a piece of paper, write down everything you're working on or juggling right now. Take note of which items are giving you the most stress. Then be honest with yourself: Which balls are ones you absolutely cannot drop? Which balls can you toss to someone else? Which can you allow yourself to drop so that someone else can learn to pick them up? Which should you never have picked up in the first place? In demystifying your responsibilities, you take back your agency and can focus on what's important to you.

If I drop the ball, I can pick it back up.

Put On Your Dancing Shoes

Dancing is an incredible way to connect with your body and allow yourself to find joy in movement. Before you start protesting that you're not the best dancer or that you have no rhythm, you should know that the only qualification for dancing is having a body!

When you dance, you give yourself the opportunity to connect mindfully with either your breath, your body, the music, or the lyrics of the song you're dancing to. The best part is that *you* get to choose which element of connection sounds the most enticing and authentic to you.

The key to exploring mindfulness through dance is *not* scrutinizing yourself and your choices. This might not come naturally to you at first, and that's totally fine. You've spent a lot of time being told to care what other people think of you, and that might take time to overcome, even when you're dancing alone. Try not to focus on how silly you think you look, or whether you're dancing "correctly." If your mind wanders, gently guide it back to your focal point of choice and dance it out.

SHAKE IT!

Good, adequate, or truly terrible—take the time to let loose and dance to your favorite tunes. Don't judge yourself. In fact, we suggest doing this away from any mirrors, just in case you're tempted to peek. (You can even close your eyes if you feel confident you won't knock anything over!) Instead, focus on reconnecting to the moment at hand. For however long the song or playlist runs, concentrate on the sound of the beat, the way your feet move on the floor, and how you feel.

I can relish the joy of movement.

Through a Magnifying Glass

Mindfulness is an investigation, and you're the lead detective. When you arrive on the scene, you don't jump to conclusions right away. Instead, you observe. You take in the world around you and meticulously break down the evidence. This allows you to see the bigger picture and learn something new. You just need to make space to do so.

When you give yourself the gift of a mindful pause, you become a master of observation: You notice where your body is holding tension, or if you need to take a deep breath. You go on a fact-finding mission, your senses acting as your guide, collecting information about the space around you and your place in it. Finally, the present clicks into place.

It is not about getting to that "aha!" moment more quickly so that you can let it pass you by and move on to the next thing. There is nothing urgent for you to solve, only clues to be gathered. Then you can move forward feeling connected to yourself and your environment. Mindfulness does not demand answers. It just asks that you shift your focus.

PEOPLE-WATCH

We're not suggesting you be a nosy neighbor, but we give you permission to people-watch. This may be different from the ways you've people-watched in the past, but don't pass judgments about the people you see or write a story about them in your head. If you feel this happening, pause and try to return to your breath. Simply reflect on what they are doing, and consider silently wishing them well as they go about their day. Pause your mental chatter and focus on something new.

I can watch and learn from the world around me.

Slow Down and Savor

How often do you find yourself eating at the kitchen counter, or bringing your dish with you to the living room so you can eat in front of the TV? Maybe you're a grab-and-go person, eating on your way to the next event, or you find yourself skipping meals because you "ran out of time."

Bestie, you deserve better than a rushed granola bar eaten between errands. Habits like this are indicators that you need to slow down. Lucky for you, meals are the perfect way to practice mindfulness because they happen every day, multiple times per day.

Make your meals mindful. You don't need to cook a twelve-course dinner all by yourself or put a ton of effort into cooking. Keep your mind on every step, even if it's just microwaving a frozen meal or ordering takeout. Use the tools you've learned thus far to single-task, focusing on the act of nourishing your body. Express gratitude for every moment.

When you're tempted to rush through what feel like life's most common, "forgettable" moments, remind yourself that you can slow down and savor each second.

SET THE TABLE

Even when you feel short on time, make mindful decisions about mealtime. If you're at work, you might choose to enjoy your lunch outside or with a co-worker rather than hunched over your desk. If you're at home, you can make it as simple as setting the table. That's right—save your emotional-support water bottle for on-the-go hydration, and take out an actual drinking glass from your cupboard instead. Light a few candles while you're at it. Focus on the task at hand and the kindness you're showing yourself. Then sit and simply enjoy the meal.

I can make everyday moments feel special.

Get a Bird's-Eye View

Imagine you're dropped into a forest, surrounded by trees. You do not know where you are or what is nearby, only that you are in the forest. If you were to climb a tree, you might be able to see more of the surrounding area immediately below, maybe even chart a path to the next lookout, where you'd repeat the process. If you were a bird (or, more realistically, if you had a drone), you'd be able to see the entire forest and surrounding area, making it easier to plan your route. What is in front of you is not the entire picture.

Anxiety and stress can cause you to get tunnel vision when it comes to what is happening around you. You can get stuck viewing the world from one, often negative, perspective. The negative feedback in your own mind begins to taint the things you care about. When this happens, it's important to gain some perspective.

Finding a new angle from which to look at your life provides an opportunity to recognize how far you've come, rather than making you feel like you're stuck in one place.

FROM ANOTHER ANGLE

In your notebook write down what is worrying you, no matter how consequential or insignificant. Try to explain what is worrying you and why it is causing you worry. (No one-word answers allowed!) When you're finished, determine which of these worries can be viewed from another angle. Rather than worrying about your performance at work, find things to praise. Rather than stressing over a first impression, think of what went well. When you view what's worrying you from a different angle, you gain a new perspective.

I can observe my worries from a new angle.

Inside Out

We don't know what we did to deserve the ability to taste chocolate, feel downy puppy fur, see an incredible work of art, hear our favorite song, or smell a bouquet of flowers. But experiencing those things sure is amazing. We've all had wonderful and not-so-pleasant sensory experiences, and they all serve to remind us that our senses are a gift.

When you're feeling stressed or anxious, there is little room for your body to feel anything else. You may even find that your physical senses have become dulled. Not to worry. You can use the senses you have at your disposal to reconnect with your body and to keep your mind from disengaging with the world around you.

Try to concentrate completely on the physical space you're in. Concentrate on the things you hear. Look around and truly take in your surroundings. Take a moment to experience the taste and smell of your cup of coffee, feel the warmth of it in your hand. When you return to your surroundings, one sense at a time, you disengage from the anxiety spiral that keeps you from experiencing the rich life you have.

COME TO YOUR SENSES

Sit somewhere comfortable and close your eyes. Start exploring what you can sense about your body, focusing on sensations like your clothes on your skin, your heartbeat, your knee that always aches after running, the smell of your detergent, the taste of your toothpaste. Then start sensing the world around you. Is the room warm? Can you hear people talking or a car driving by? Can you smell someone cooking dinner? Use your senses to explore from the inside out.

When I focus, I can feel things more vividly.

Slow and Steady

When you watch dancers performing an intricate piece of choreography or a pair of stunt doubles carrying out an intense fight scene, the moves can seem almost too fast to keep up with. You watch the tangle of limbs, wondering how the performers are keeping the moves straight, let alone acting in sync with one another. Here's their secret: They took it slow at first.

You might even know what we're talking about from taking a dance class (or learning pop-star moves in front of your TV). While learning the choreography, performers start at half-speed. They'll practice little pieces of the dance, count by count. And then, once they're comfortable, they'll do the full dance and take it at full speed.

We can learn a thing or two from these performers. Our day-to-day is an intricate dance that we have choreographed over time. There are some parts we speed through, and others we could probably take more slowly. Is there something in your life you've been speeding through when you really need to slow down? Remember, there is no rush to "get it right."

I can slow everything down to focus on me.

TAKE IT AT HALF-SPEED

The rush of everyday life can make you feel like there is no time to be mindful. You're juggling too much, moving too quickly, and unable to find a space to pause. Fine! You don't need to pause. You can just slow down. Today, when you feel yourself rushing, take whatever you're doing at half-speed. Heck, you can even be late today if you need to. (Sorry to whoever you have plans with!) Feel what it's like to take your time and focus on the task at hand with intention.

Your Body, at Rest

Your body tells a rich story of the things you carry. When you're moving, you may not notice the strain or stress. Rest gives you a great opportunity to listen to your body.

Keeping your body moving for too long is like being in a loud room and trying to carry on a conversation with a friend. With music playing and other people around you having conversations, you might catch only every other word or miss the nuance of their reactions. If you two have that same conversation at home, in quiet and comfort, you'll be able to see and hear them more clearly. The conversation takes on new meaning.

When was the last time you paid attention to your body at rest? Think about how you sit at your work computer or on the couch watching TV. How do you hold your body? Do you sprawl out, taking up as much space as possible in the name of comfort? Or is your tension keeping you tightly wound? Note how your shoulders hold stress or how your hands fidget. Your body at rest tells the story of your stress. When you hear that story, you can address it.

GET THE WIGGLES OUT

You can complete this exercise lying on the floor, sitting in a chair, or even standing up. Take a few deep breaths. Then get a case of the wiggles. Shake out your entire body, bestie! Shake your feet and your ankles. Your legs, your arms, and your head. Feel the sensations as you do—what feels good? What's feeling not so fun? Then, body part by body part, find stillness. Observe what you feel when you're still versus when you're moving. Do not judge either state; simply take it in.

I can shake out the tension and find stillness.

Check Your Screen Time

Phones are part of our daily lives, and—no matter how often you threaten to throw yours into the nearest body of water—they're not going anywhere. This isn't an anti-phone rant; our phones do an incredible job of broadening our horizons and showing us corners of the world we might not have seen otherwise.

But here's the thing, bestie: There's a whole lot to experience in *your* corner of the world. You've got to strike a balance. When your head is in your lap, looking down at your phone, you're probably not getting a good look at the world around you. Not to mention, no one wants "tech neck," okay?

We're not saying you can never scroll on your phone again, or that you need to delete your social media and go off the grid. We just want you to look up once in a while! Spend a few mindful minutes per day disconnected and see what you can discover. There are so many things to be found in the world around you if you make the effort to find stillness and become a mindful observer.

BE A PHONE-FREE SPIRIT

See how many minutes you can go without your phone today. We mean totally *without! No "just checking" your email or scrolling through socials as a "break." At the end of the day, mark the number of phone-free minutes you were able to accomplish in your journal. Now think about adding more phone-free time! How many more minutes can you do tomorrow? The next day? These moments add up to hours, then days, and so on and so forth. Keep track of how much time you've gained back.*

I own my screens. They don't own my focus.

Mindful Mornings

Morning people know the power of getting up while the world is still quiet. Maybe that's you, and maybe it is absolutely not. That's okay! Morning person or not, the moments before the whole house wakes up or before you rush yourself out the door are the perfect chance to connect with yourself and make mindfulness a priority.

No need to start waking up hours before the sun rises. Just set your alarm for a few minutes earlier tomorrow morning. (Don't hit "snooze"!) Spend those minutes connecting to yourself and the world around you. Watch the light filter in through the windows, savor the smell of your coffee brewing, feel the weight of your blanket, hear the birds chirping.

Though it's possible to practice mindfulness all day long, you're not required to. You can weave moments of presence into your routine and remind yourself that you *get* to experience another day. Before you go through all that the day brings, experience the peace and comfort of knowing you can be present for every second of it.

CATCH A SUNRISE

Wake up early one day this week and make it a point to catch the sunrise. You don't need to suddenly become a person who consistently wakes up while it's dark out. But think of this is as a chance to experience the quiet assurance of a new day without distractions or obligations. Start your day knowing that you have a new chance to connect with yourself on a deeper, more mindful level.

Each new day brings a chance to connect.

It's Time to Celebrate

Celebrations are times where we mark our joy (and declare it boldly!) with parties, gifts, and praise. Think of a celebration you've recently attended. Whether it was a birthday, wedding, or another milestone, you set aside a date on the calendar to connect with others. Maybe you even took the time to reflect on a relationship through writing a card or giving a speech, or perhaps you expressed your joy with dancing.

What if you didn't limit yourself to life's "big moments" to celebrate? Instead, what if you reflected on life's smaller moments and celebrated them through mindfulness? When you do this, you automatically create space to be present and encourage yourself to look for joy and abundance.

Look to infuse celebration into the small, seemingly insignificant parts of your day. By turning simple, everyday actions into a celebration, you develop a habit of mindfully pausing and reframing.

This practice isn't about *pretending* that everything around you is perfect. It's about choosing to take a mindful minute to appreciate what's going right, *right now*. Life isn't made up of milestones; it's made up of moments, and you have the power to recognize each of them.

DON'T WAIT FOR A MILESTONE

You're kind of a big deal, and so is everything you do. And we mean everything. *Make a habit of celebrating yourself. Choose one thing you did successfully today and pat yourself on the back, bestie. Celebrating can look like smiling to yourself, writing down your experience, or even going to dinner with friends. No matter what your celebration looks like, honor yourself in a way that makes you feel joy. Focusing on these wins reminds you that there's so much worth celebrating when you pay attention.*

I can make a big deal out of small things.

Acknowledge Your World

If you've ever hung out with a toddler who is expanding their vocabulary, you've noticed they simply call it like they see it—out loud for everyone to hear. When they see a cat, they exclaim, "KITTY!" The same goes for a truck, a leaf, or a trash can. There's no stopping them from sharing all the words they know and all the things they see. They acknowledge the world around them with wonder and joy and encourage their grown-ups to do the same.

At some point, we stopped performing this ritual (and not just because shouting all the things we see as adults is frowned on). We don't even name the things we're seeing to ourselves in our heads. Our busy lives keep our eyes on our phones and our thoughts on so much more than what is around us.

Anxiety and overwhelm can also trick you into thinking you're not seeing the world for what it is. When you're moving so quickly, your life can begin to feel like one big blur. It's time to connect back to that childlike wonder and take in the world around you, seeking connection and joy.

NAME IT ALL

Find a comfortable, distraction-free place to sit. Close your eyes and take a few deep breaths, relaxing into your chair a little bit more with each one. When you're ready, open your eyes and look around the room. As you take in your environment and your gaze lands on different objects, name them out loud. Allow your eyes to linger where they want. Do this for as long as it takes to feel like you've quieted your mind and returned to the present moment.

The world around me is beautiful. I will acknowledge it.

Put a Lid on It

Okay, we know that the title can come off a *little* harsh, but hear us out!

There's a reason for lids. They help keep things contained and organized, and they keep the mess from spilling out and getting all over the place. Consider laundry hampers or trash cans. When they don't have a lid, you can easily overstuff them, leading to their contents spilling all over the floor and making more work for you in the long run. A lid is a reminder that there is only so much that this vessel can hold.

Your mind is the vessel of your thoughts—the good, bad, and anxious. There is only so much it can comfortably hold. When you're feeling stressed or overwhelmed, your thoughts and feelings can quickly begin to spill over.

We are *not* advocating that you use a mental lid to push down and ignore your feelings. Rather, a lid can look like a mindful pause or releasing some worries to make room for peace. The lid encourages you to recognize you're at capacity, relieving some of your stress and overwhelm.

I can release my worries to make room for joy.

BOX UP YOUR WORRIES

Create a "worry box" that you can keep on your desk or at home. This box is a place to put all your worries as they come, giving you a tool to release them instead of focusing and fixating on them. When you're having anxious thoughts or feeling stressed, write your worries on a strip of paper, and then release them into the "worry box." If you'd rather not keep a physical box, you can start a list on your phone or in your journal.

Dip Your Brush

Imagine life as a painting, and you're the painter. (Put aside any qualms you have about your artistic ability; it's just a metaphor, bestie!) There are times when each stroke is steady and sure; you feel in control and capable. Other times, the brush runs dry, or you're not quite sure what you should do next. These moments can feel stressful or confusing. One thing is for sure: You don't want an unfinished painting. The next step is always, *always* dipping your brush back into the paint and starting again.

Each breath you take is another chance to dip your brush into more paint, to refill and let it go onto the paper. Don't judge the marks you make; they paint a full picture of who you are.

Your breath is kind of like that paintbrush. And the beautiful thing about your breath is that it's always there for you. You can't lose it, and even if you forget it's there (which is to be expected, as we often take it for granted), you can always return to it. You can return to your breath, reset, refresh, and continue to create something beautiful.

DRAW YOUR BREATH

You're going to draw your breath. Grab some paper and something to write with. Take a few deep breaths in and out, noticing how quickly or slowly you are breathing. Place your pen on the paper and draw a line (this can look however you want it to) on your inhale and another on your exhale. Repeat as you breathe. Try changing the speed of your breath. How does that change the lines you're drawing? They don't have to be straight lines, and the length doesn't matter. Simply breathe in and out, and draw.

I can always draw a new breath.

Cooking Up Something Good

Chaos is the main ingredient on every American baking competition show. There are multiple contestants running around checking their ovens and whipping up icings. And there's always a secret ingredient, a special twist, and time limits that would have the average home baker shaking in their oven mitts.

But for all its chaos, the contestants somehow remain calm enough to measure correctly, ice with precision, roll out fondant for decorations, and answer the judges as they ask them questions mid-process.

Their secret to staying calm, cool, and collected? Concentrate on one step of the recipe at a time. A baker cannot make a batter without cracking eggs. They can't ice the cake before it is out of the oven and cooled down.

You cannot see the future before you face the present. The world can be a chaotic place, but you've got this, bestie. You can trust yourself to remain calm, cool, and collected. Your secret ingredient? Mindfulness. When you focus on completing one step at a time, your mind stays malleable and your eyes stay focused on what's in front of you, instead of what's to come.

A RECIPE FOR MINDFULNESS

Are you the kind of person who has an archive of recipes you'd like to make "someday"? Well, we have great news: Today is someday! Choose a recipe you're excited about and make it. The trick? Give the process your full, undiluted attention. This may sound simple enough, but cooking without getting distracted can be challenging. Give yourself grace, keep chopping or frying or boiling, and try not to let your mind wander too far. Then enjoy the fruits of your mindfulness! It's the secret ingredient.

When I focus, I appreciate the work.

Catch and Release

Have you ever watched someone fish for fun? They don't go out onto the water and try to catch every fish in the lake. People who fish dedicate time to sitting on the shore or in a boat with their line cast out, and they practice patience. They don't judge themselves if they aren't catching anything. Some days the fish are biting, and other days the lake seems like it's empty.

If you observe someone fishing, you'll notice they rarely keep every fish they catch. They usually throw quite a few back. That's because there are certain rules they must follow. There might be a limit to how many fish they can take home, or maybe they can keep only fish of a certain size or type, or they're just fishing for fun.

You can treat your thoughts like those fish: Catch them. Reel them in and look at them. You can throw back what doesn't serve you. You can measure a thought and decide that it's not big enough to hold on to—or maybe it's too big to hold for very long. Keep only what you need.

REEL IN YOUR THOUGHTS

Sit comfortably in a quiet place and focus on your breathing. Try to clear your mind. While you sit in silence, you may find that you become distracted. That's okay! When a thought comes up, imagine yourself catching it with a fishing rod and reeling it in. Then imagine yourself releasing it rather than dwelling on it. We know you've got a lot of thoughts, so this may feel difficult at first. You don't need to sit in silence for hours; start with a few minutes. Extend this meditative practice little by little.

I can practice release and learn to let go.

Sing It Out

Did you know that singing is known to lower cortisol, the stress hormone? We're not even kidding; it's science. When you sing, you feel less lonely, less negative, and more connected to others. You may also get a much-needed endorphin boost, which can leave you feeling happy and confident. That sounds like a win to us.

And please don't say you "can't sing." I bet your car, your shower, and even your cat would be quick to point out otherwise. You can sing (whatever it sounds like) and reap the benefits, even if you're not the most technically perfect singer. Moving on!

Singing is also an awesome way to approach mindfulness. When you sing, you devote so much mental space to the activity that you shut down that voice in your head that's been talking a mile a minute.

As you sing, you may even recognize some of the mindfulness skills you've learned already: Focusing on your breath, accepting your emotions, allowing your thoughts to pass by, and speaking positively to yourself. Now what are we singing?

I can do everything with feeling.

THE SHOWER POWER BALLAD

Pick your Shower Power Ballad. This is a song you can return to, time and time again—one you sing in the shower to remind yourself that you are strong and awesome and cannot be tamed. Bonus points if there's a sick air-guitar riff or an eighties drum machine. Take time choosing the song that connects you most to who you are at your core. Listen and really hear the lyrics. Finally, no matter how terrible you think you are at singing, just sing!

Halt the Grind

These days, people love to glorify the "grind." No doubt you've seen people on your social media feeds humble-bragging about being "locked in" and doing a five-to-nine before their nine-to-five (waking up at five a.m. and hustling until they start work at nine a.m.).

Before being co-opted by the internet, the word "grind" described a boring, day-to-day routine, or the act of taking something big and making it smaller and smaller (like what happens to peppercorns when you use a pepper mill). Now the work has taken on a new persona—something you *must* do to keep up with everyone else. And so often these days, "the grind" involves adding *more* to your plate, giving you another thing to focus on, to crush, to dominate.

But when you spend your life grinding away, you take something big and beautiful and diminish it down to dust.

Repeat after us: *No more grind*. You are way too awesome and way too special to be constantly grinding, rushing through life, and missing out. You can work hard and meet your goals while taking time to remind yourself why you're even working toward those things in the first place.

Recognize and Reset

Identify the moments during your day when you find yourself rushing. Note them when you feel them. These are the perfect times to slow down or take an intentional pause. This practice sounds counterintuitive because you probably feel like you're rushing for a reason. But taking a second to slow down can help you break a pattern of stress and overwhelm. When you begin to pause in the middle of the rush, you give yourself permission to take your time and take it all in.

I don't need to rush; I have all I need.

Dive In

Imagine yourself floating in a calm ocean when suddenly the water becomes rough. You came to relax, but now that feels impossible. You might be tempted to leave the water, to cede that domain to the waves and let them change your plans.

Stress, anxiety, and overwhelm want you to live a life where you're reacting to what's happening on the surface, often all at once. On the surface, every splash feels like a tsunami, every ripple is a great disturbance.

What if, instead of choosing to leave the ocean, you decided to go for a swim? Under the water, the world becomes less loud, less abrasive. Mindfulness invites you to experience the quiet that can come underneath all the noise.

When you take a deep breath and go beneath the surface, you can focus on the feeling of the water around you and the sensation of the air in your lungs. The world slows down as you experience it from a different angle. You won't always be able to escape the noise, but when you look to go deeper and reconnect with yourself, you can find peace among the waves.

BREATHE DEEP

Find a comfortable position to lie down flat (you can use a yoga mat or even do this in bed). Take a deep breath in and feel your chest fill with air. Notice the way your breath creates space in your body. Experience the sensation of your back against the floor (or mattress). Stay in this position, releasing your breath. Notice where your body is touching the floor. Can you feel yourself relaxing and sinking deeper into the position? Repeat this as many times as you'd like, focusing on the sensations of your body.

I can go deeper, no matter the waves.

How Are You, Really?

In American culture, "How are you?" is more of a greeting than a sincere question. When you pass a co-worker in the hall and they ask how you are while you're both on the way to separate meetings, you aren't really expected to stop and tell them how you're *actually* doing. Too often, the answer is a simple "Fine, thanks!" or a cheesy "Living the dream!" Even when you respond, "Good, and you?" neither of you stop to chat about the answer.

When was the last time you were asked that question and answered it honestly? How are you, *really*?

The tendency to push everything down and pretend it's all fine, to gloss over life's hard moments and keep them to yourself, is a common response to stress and overwhelm. Even thinking or talking about your actual emotions can feel exhausting. But friend, we genuinely want to know how you are.

So take a deep breath, and ask yourself that question. Close your eyes and let your thoughts surface. Don't judge them or push them aside. Let yourself think them. Then release them. Accept that this is you, in this moment.

ASK IT AND MEAN IT

Choose one person you interact with today and ask them, "How are you?" Then allow them to respond. Pause and make yourself available for conversation, inviting them to give you a real answer. Mindfully listen to how they are. Watch their facial expressions as they answer. Look for their verbal and nonverbal cues. Be intentional with your attention and responses. Becoming a better listener helps you to become more mindful with the people around you.

I find meaning in intentional interactions.

Out of Touch

Think of the term "out of touch." We know it has kind of a negative connotation. It might bring up a lot of feelings for you. No one *wants* to be out of touch, but at its core, being "out of touch" just means you've been paying attention to the wrong things.

It's like watching a movie or a play and only paying attention to the background actors in every scene. You'll miss the whole plot!

Do you ever feel like your stress and overwhelm are leading you to feel out of touch? You're hurrying along from one moment to the next, never stopping to take in how you're feeling or what's going on around you, and when you eventually look up, you feel like you've lost the plot. You may feel like you're always asking yourself, *When did* that *happen?*

What you need are touchpoints, mindful moments you plan to pick your head up, look around, and shift your focus. These touchpoints can happen every day, every week, or every month. Check in with yourself, your family, your friends. Don't let stress steal your focus.

FEEL IT OUT

Using your sense of touch, create a mindful moment for yourself. Choose an object with an interesting texture—your pet's fur, a rock, a piece of sandpaper, a blanket. In a distraction-free environment, close your eyes, and focus completely on how it feels to touch that object. Name what you feel as you do: soft, fluffy, smooth, rough, cold, hot. When other thoughts come up, don't get frustrated. Simply do your best to return to the sensations and continue to get specific about what you're feeling.

I can touch and feel my way through the world.

Go Solo

Sometimes what's keeping us from being our best, most mindful selves is other people. It's not that your friends and family don't *want* you to be mindful. But when there are other voices in the room, other opinions to be listened to, and other desires to be met, it's easy for you to follow along. This is especially true if you're stressed or overwhelmed. It can feel easier to go on autopilot and ignore how you're feeling.

This is not a call to cut off your friends and family. You need a community! But if you want to take your mindfulness to the next level, you must make time to be alone. You might be thinking, *I do things on my own all the time,* and we're sure you do. But doing those things mindfully is a whole new ballgame, bestie!

When you get yourself alone, you can make space to check in with yourself. You can step away from the noise, silence the group chats, and breathe deep. You've worked hard so far, gaining a new awareness of yourself. Don't let it slip away into the noise!